Worlds Beyond the World

The Fantastic Vision of William Morris

Richard Mathews

R. REGINALD
THE Borgo Press
SAN BERNARDINO, CALIFORNIA
MCMLXXVIII

To Julie

Library of Congress Cataloging in Publication Data:

Mathews, Richard, 1944-
 Worlds beyond the world.

   (Popular writers of today; v. 13) (The Milford series)
   Bibliography: p. 63.
   1.   Morris, William, 1834-1896—Criticism and interpretation.
I. Title.
PR5084.M296   823′.8   78-247
ISBN 0-89370-218-8

Copyright © 1978 by Richard Mathews.
All rights reserved. No part of this book may be reproduced in any form without the expressed written consent of the publisher. Printed in the United States of America by Griffin Printing & Lithograph Co., Glendale, CA.

Produced, designed, and published by R. Reginald, The Borgo Press, P.O. Box 2845, San Bernardino, CA 92406. Typesetting by Mary A. Burgess. Paste-up by Holly Sullivan. Cover design by Judy Cloyd.

First Edition———May, 1978

1. WORLDS BEYOND THE WORLD

In fantasy the human mind builds worlds beyond the world. By showing us a glimpse of unrealized possibilities, the fantasy writer sheds a wondrous, glowing light on the known world, helping us to see the familiar with new clarity. While all good literature involves fantasy to some extent, the form, theme, and even the language used to express these "worlds beyond" did not take shape until the late nineteenth century, nearly 200 years after the first English novel.

English fantasy literature begins with William Morris. There are streams and sources of many kinds contributing to the flow of literary fantasy in English, but Morris is the common influence cited by the most important pioneers in the mode—C. S. Lewis, Lord Dunsany, James Branch Cabell, J. R. R. Tolkien, and many others. Looking beyond present history to the distant past, particularly to the Middle Ages, Morris found simple, direct and epic exercise of imagination unbound by realistic conventionality. He noted with sadness that even the language had changed since the early days when "everybody who could express himself at all did so beautifully, was a poet for that occasion, because all language was beautiful." In his day as in ours commercial advertising, political manipulation, and journalistic sensationalism led Morris to recognize that "now language is utterly degraded in our daily lives, and poets have to make a new tongue each for himself." Building on the strong emotion and idealism of the Romantics, and the growing popularity of the novel, Morris looked beyond his age to the future as he evolved the fantasy form, written in a "new tongue," full of details and challenges which reflect our own mundane existence, but which lift us beyond our day-to-day lives. Morris believed that the best art should "tell of men's aspirations for more than material life can give them," and hoped to create a fiction which could raise life to the level of heroism. In his fictional worlds beyond the world he unveils a realm of Platonic Ideals embodying Romantic hopes in concrete terms. Heaven is replaced with a host of alternatives, recognizably human in scale, realizable here on earth.

Morris's fiction attempts to instill a new attitude in the mind of the reader. It is a consistent, specific attitude toward decent human values and an appreciation for quality in life. All of his work is utopian in at least one dimension, in that it seeks to ennoble the thoughts, sentiments, and aspirations of men. But this ennobling quality is elusive and very difficult to talk about. Though it becomes clearer with every reading, more definitely a central part of the purpose of his work and the success of his literary achievement, it is practically impossible to discuss within the parameters of conventional criticism.

Anyone writing about Morris is faced with a problem of methodology. An *Athenoeum* critic reviewing one of his earliest fantasy novels spoke about needing new canons of criticism to discuss these works. Northrup Frye's brilliant collection of essays, *Fables of Identity*, makes substantial contributions to a critical methodology serviceable for the mainstream of English literature; his *Anatomy of Criticism* presents critical assumptions which can structure a comprehensive methodology. Some of that structure, an archetypal approach built upon the shoulders of the best New Critical methods, is appropriate and illuminating when discussing the fantasy novels. Freudian and Jungian psychology combined with Frye's methods will yield even more interesting analysis. This is surely part of the reason for Frye's recognition that Morris "should not be left on the sidelines of prose fiction merely because the critic has not learned to take the romance form seriously."

The need now is for a look at all of Morris's fiction as a body of work—distinctive, original, and consistent. The stylistic invention and depth of his mythography are different from, yet comparable to, the achievement of William Blake in poetry or William Faulkner in his Yoknapatawpha County myths. Considering both the aim and achievement of Morris's fiction, it is fitting to subject it to the quality demands of the New Critics (including Frye) with regard to its worth as finely crafted literature. It is also appropriate to consider its psychological and social vision with regard to Freud, Jung, and Marx, for it clearly embodies the content of many of their theories, and tries to envision positive examples of psychologically well-integrated human beings and socially-politically well-constituted societies.

Blake's poetry helped us to see "a world in a grain of sand. . . And eternity in an hour." Morris constructs his parallel worlds beyond this world not so much to grasp infinity or eternity (more often the object of the science fiction writer than the fantacist) as to inspire the heroic hopes and united spirit of a people here and now. He is, perhaps, closer to Faulkner's conviction that man will not merely endure, but prevail. It takes a great deal of time for us to understand these matters individually—time to read slowly and grasp the alternatives these fantasy novels provoke—and a great deal more time and space than I have at my disposal to encompass them critically and intellectually. It does seem very clear to me that Morris's fiction has been tremendously underrated in literature classes, while it has been stubbornly read by a popular audience buying copies from drugstore, bus station, and airport paperback racks; and these very non-scholars are the audience Morris would most have wanted. They intuitively recognize the importance of the imagination and the joy of his work, and they need not belabor it, like those of us who feel compelled to explain the world of books to itself.

Richard Mathews
Gulfport, Florida
February, 1978

1. INTO THE UNKNOWN

William Morris was familiar with worlds beyond the everyday world of his relatively conventional English middle class upbringing from the time his parents first let him wander through the woods of nearby Epping Forest. His childhood was lived in an active and imaginative way, and the curious ability to integrate fact, act, and fantasy seems to have been with him from the first. Wandering beyond his nearby forest, he discovered the ancient stone monuments of Tilsbury and Stonehenge, and through them the history of the ancient days in Britain; but these facts served only to flesh out and make more real the rich life of the Middle Ages, a life which grew more clear with each passing year in his imagination. He saw himself as a knight on a charger, roaming the woods in quest of adventure and enlightenment, aiming to set the world to rights, to free whatever prisoners might be suffering at the hands of a cruel and evil tyrant. The woods served as the entrance to the unknown world from his youngest years.

Public school education in England was not much help to Morris, and he always retained a dim view of formal education; but he did avidly pursue learning independently. He read widely and studied as much as he could about the earliest history and archaeology of his country, and he came to know a great deal about the English Gothic style. In 1851 he left Marlborough School to be tutored for Oxford by the Rev. F. B. Guy, and in the space of a year, challenged by Guy's mind and ideals and naturally attracted to epic literature, Morris developed into a fair classical scholar. He was admitted to Oxford in January of

1853 with the intention of taking holy orders. In his first years there he established close relationships with Edward Burne-Jones, Charles Faulkner, Richard Dixon, William Fulford, and Cormell Price, and through them became increasingly aware of current politics, literature, and the arts. It was there that he first read Chaucer and Malory and Thorpe's *Northern Mythlogy*, and first came to know the visual art of the Pre-Raphaelite painters, drawn by Ruskin's assessment of them: "Pre-Raphaelitism has but one principle, that of absolute, uncompromising truth in all that it does. . . ."

Morris learned from the Pre-Raphaelites, particularly Dante Gabriel Rossetti, and his painter friend Burne-Jones, to see with the eye of an artist. He trained himself as a designer, and applied his imaginative designs to a wide variety of materials. He became the foremost visionary of his time partly because his eye for detail and pattern combined with his awareness of both small and large structural elements in an effort to create a whole which would be both aesthetically and conceptually true. Like most of the Pre-Raphaelites with whom he is now linked, Morris believed in a near-surrealist attention to detail. This fact of his writing is often overlooked by those critics who note the more dominant overall purpose and design of each story; but it nonetheless remains the foundations of his fantastic imagination. As in his designs for fabric and wallpapers, Morris relies in the patterning of his fiction upon the pleasing repetition of detail—patterns of imagery, symbol, and archetype—and he also utilizes shapes which are recognizable as coming from the real world, but which in *his* work became abstracted, idealized, or in simple terms, well "designed."

His sense of design brought him into intimate contact with a variety of media, and it is noteworthy that he sought designs peculiar and appropriate to each of the media in which he worked. One of the amazing things about Morris was his ability to work through problems of both subject and execution in his head; consequently, he often created his designs at first attempt in polished and finished form. He had a similar facility with poetry. When he first began reading his work to his Oxford friends, they were delighted, and his reaction to their praise was: "If this is poetry, it is very easy to write." Later critics continue to praise the maturity and completion Morris brought to both literature and art from the beginning. He left only one surviving oil painting, his first effort, painted just after he left Oxford; it hangs today in a prominent place in the Tate Gallery, in London.

It is not much of an exaggeration to look upon Morris as a founder of the modern art movement in England, and that claim, made on the strength of his work as a designer, is true in many ways of his fiction as well. When he turned to the written medium, he sensed from the first that his greatest achievements would be found not in imitative representational art, but in a much more conceptual and abstract fictive design. He felt that words should not be used merely to construct a literary reality imitating the mundane world—this denigrated language. It was using words merely as imitation, never allowing the language itself to take on the power, colors, and form inherent in the medium. Words employed in the purest way could create a reality quite apart form the ordinary. They could be decorative and beautiful *in themselves*; only by removing the distracting belief that literature should imitate reality, a belief which had been assumed by most writers and critics since Aristotle, could Morris hope to revolutionize fiction in much the same way that he sought to revolutionize society. With new vision and new forms, it was his belief that the neoteric breakthrough would occur through a recognition of the special reality and vitality peculiar to artistic imagination.

During the great upswelling of creativity which poured from Morris during his undergraduate years, and which paved the way for all of his future development as an artist-author, he laid the groundwork for what would be a new and revolutionary direction for the novel. In the short stories first published in the *Oxford and Cambridge Magazine* he introduced both a general approach and a great theme; and it remained only for his mastery of his own style, and the refinement of his social vision, for his worlds beyond the world to come fully into view.

THE STORY OF THE UNKNOWN CHURCH

Morris published his first short story in January, 1856, when he was 22. He and his friend Edward Burne-Jones had decided they would dedicate themselves to bettering the world through art instead of pursuing the religious careers they both had originally intended. In fact, art became for them a kind of religion, and they talked of forming a "Brotherhood" to enact their artistic dreams. *The Oxford and Cambridge Magazine* was the first tangible result of the new dedication, and was carried out by the "brothers" as a method of expressing their new faith that art, literature, criticism, and social reform were part and parcel of the same enterprise. Thus, Morris's first story, "The Story of the Unknown Church," is significant in alluding to the church career which Morris never came to know, and in substituting art for religion as the best method to celebrate, explore, and convey the unknown.

Clearly, it was not "known" realities which interested Morris. It was the world beyond, the unexplained, the mysterious. The story is told by the master mason of a church built more than 600 years ago. The sense of mystery is associated with the veils of time which separate this supernatural narrator from present reality, and also with the fabric of the ancient building itself, the *structure* which has received a speaking and transcendent shape through the power of the craftsman's hand. Appearing in the initial issue of the magazine which Morris financed and edited, "The Story of the Unknown Church" was the first of eight short stories pubished there anonymously—the only short stories Morris ever wrote—and it started his involvement with fantasy writing, serving to clarify and direct his imaginative energies.

The influences and echoes of his favorite college reading—the Teutonic mythology of Jacob and Wilhelm Grimm, Norse myth and legend, Malory, early English metrical romance, and even Edgar Allen Poe—are strongly evident in this early work, but Morris stamps the tales with the unmistakable imprint of his own style. They are lyrical, impressionist fictions compared to the nearly epic proportions of his later work, but they clearly stake out the terrain he intends to explore. As he evolved from a young man with deep religious commitments through a mature exercise of his literary art and craft to an older man with deep aesthetic, social, and human commitments, Morris's fiction altered and expanded. The early stories are obsessed with death. Many of the central characters engage in bloody battle or are brought to a sudden and disorienting confrontation with violent ends. The encounter is usually abrupt and discontinuous, and partly because the fictional form itself is brief, the consequences cannot be dealt with gradually, in slow adjustment, but must be faced immediately as a crisis or shock. The individual characters seem relatively powerless in the face of death, mere pawns in the play of the cosmic forces (fate or its equivalent) which define and control the circumstances. The presence of religion in nearly all the tales is striking, and is almost always associated with tombs, murders, or mortality.

Not until much later in life, with his first longer work of fiction, *A Dream of*

John Ball, does Morris create a satisfactory alternative to the disturbing environments of the early stories. There for the first time we encounter a preacher unconcerned with an afterlife (the afterlife is the primary world-beyond-the-world of traditional religion, and is the most obvious other-worldly touchstone in the stories). Ball is directing his message to the continuity of generations on earth, hoping to improve the future with his work and sacrifice. Thereafter in Morris's fiction, organized religion does not appear anywhere near so frequently, and death is presented as a natural part of the life process, instead of being the central concern. Beginning in the early fictions, then, we can watch a shift from fairly conventional religious anxieties and moral imperatives— a matrix of rules in which the individual is caught—toward a creative vision of self-determination, where individual characters increasingly control their own destinies while they shape society toward embodiment of their ideals.

Even these short stories show Morris depicting pattern and type rather than individualized psychological character studies. He disliked the contemporary tendency to so-called "subtle psychology and abrupt formless methods," preferring the qualities he found in medieval literature: "rude joviality, and simple and direct delineation of character." His own writing develops these attitudes by portraying characters through action in the context of a "parallel world," a separate reality vastly distant from our own in either space or time, in customs or language. Through the use of pattern or archetype, we can easily perceive parallels with our own circumstances. This makes his fiction at once an escape from the tyranny of the day-to-day world, and a chance to explore ideals in a context approaching the higher plane Plato suggested when he spoke of Ideal Forms.

In "The Unknown Church," the dead first-person narrator speaks of a church which "vanished from the face of the earth," but his story is told within the context of a bountiful and beautiful earth, which forever renews itself through new growths of flowers and foliage. The plenitude of internal patterning takes place within a circle of nature, present in this tale symbolically as a grove of poplar trees within which the church is built. Morris details the trees, saying they seem to speak, though in a synaesthesia of visual pattern rather than human speech: "And whenever a wind passed over them, were it ever so little a breath, it set them all a-ripple; and when the wind was high, they bowed and swayed very low, and the wind, as it lifted the leaves, and showed their silvery white sides, or as again in the lulls of it, it let them drop, kept on changing the trees from green to white, and white to green. . . . "

The narrator recalls one particular autumn when all the figures on the west front of the church had been finished, except for a statue of Abraham which he was to complete himself. The mason can only think of Abraham in process (like the church), in movement (like the poplars), not as a static, finished work: "I could not think of him sitting there, quiet and solemn, while the Judgement-Trumpet was being blown; I rather thought of him as he looked when he chased those kings so far; riding far ahead of any of his company, with his mail-hood off his head, and lying in grim folds down his back, with the strong west wind blowing his wild black hair far out behind him." In the mason's view of the hero, the Biblical myth is not allowed to dominate the fresh force of imagination. The mason's mind is drawn from contemplation of the Biblical subject into a realistically human view of Abraham in action. Even as he watches Abraham in his mind's eye, "he leapt, horse and man, into a deep river, quiet, swift, and smooth." The vanishing of the vision parallels the vanishing church and narrator, and is part of an emerging pattern of disappeance and transformation which

7

we encounter again and again in the shifting realities of Morrisian fantasy. He most often makes the transition through a familiar symbol of flux and purification—water—which in this story is given the addition of flowers (stressing the fertile, feminine aspect of water): "And there was something in the moving of the water-lilies as the breast of the horse swept them aside, that suddenly took away the thought of Abraham and brought a strange dream of lands I had never seen. . . ." The narrator is overcome by a great thirst, but as soon as he touches the water of the river to his lips, the scenery disappears and changes (once again, water is an image of transformation): he finds himself flat on his back in a boat staring at a blue sky and a dark cliff with a castle on it.

With an eye for detail that is nearly cinematic, Morris zooms in on the castle itself: "On one of the towers, growing in a cranny of the worn stones, a great bunch of golden and blood-red wall-flowers." A man on the battlements tosses a handful of these flowers over the edge and they fall in the boat beside the narrator. "In my dream," he tells us, "I could see even very far off things much clearer than we see real material things on the earth." The story is the fictional equivalent of a Pre-Raphaelite painting. The details form the pattern and the structure of the composition without concession to conventional assumptions about perspectives; and the details are charged with unexplained significance. As he watches, the flags change on the castle (a signal that the ruler has changed), and the displaced flag is thrown, like Abraham, the narrator, and the flowers, into the river. This final image of loss and change prompts the narrator to begin his own story of loss: he describes the death of his sister and her betrothed, his best friend, Amyot. It has been the loss of these loved ones which has prompted the mason to construct his loving tomb canopy as monument "carved all about with many flowers and histories."

Near the end, a final detail is rendered with magnificent clarity: "I do not know what time of the day it was, but I know that it was a glorious autumn day, a day soft with melting, golden haze: a vine and a rose grew together, and trailed half across the window, so that I could not see much of the beautiful sky, and nothing of the town or country beyond; the vine leaves were touched with red here and there, and three over-blown roses, light pink roses, hung amongst them. I remember dwelling on the strange lines the autumn had made in red on one of the gold-green vine leaves, and watching one leaf of one of the over-blown roses, expecting it to fall every minute." In the image of the over-blown rose, Morris encapsulates an eloquent figure for death as the mother of beauty. All things will change and give place. And the death of the lovers prompts the sculptor to carve their gorgeous tomb. Even the sculptor's life is seen as a part of the process, "till one morning, quite early, when they came into the church for matins, they found me lying dead, with my chisel in my hand, underneath the last lily of the tomb."

There are parallel worlds and parallel realities in the patterns here. The effect of the whole is like a nest of Chinese boxes, box within box, depicting the changing vitality of life and the enduring eloquence of art. Within the story, the tiny line of autumn red lacing the gold-green vine leaves is a microscopic version of the tale which the passage of time writes upon the larger canvas of the world, and which the author chisels in the stone he is carving. "The Story of the Unknown Church" is a lyrical hymn to the power of art, as it celebrates the eternity of beauty shining through the repetition of change. The final irony, of course, is that we have known from the first sentence that even the art embodied in this church has disappeared completely into the ruins of time, and "no one knows now even where it stood."

LINDENBORG POOL

In marked contrast to the active beauties of change in his first story, "Lindenborg Pool" presents the horror of stagnation, and stasis is characterized as the ultimate evil. Pattern demands movement over time or space, for without multiplicity and repetition the notion of pattern cannot exist. In his designs for wallpapers and fabrics Morris directly faced the problem of "repeats" in the pattern, and believed them to be of central concern to the designer. He felt they should be frequent enough to establish the firm overall structure (or pattern), but not so close as to become obvious, distracting, or overpowering. These same concerns were constantly in mind as he developed literary designs, and the unadulterated drab eternity represented by the unchanging Lindenborg Pool is the antithesis of the elements of beauty-through-change that he celebrated in so many literary and artistic inventions. Like the first tale, the focus is on death, but a contrast is clearly seen in the plant imagery of the second story: "All round the edges of it [the pool] grew a rank crop of dreary reeds and segs, some round, some flat, but none ever flowering as other things flowered, never dying and being renewed, but always the same stiff array of unbroken reeds and segs, some round, some flat." Even the repetition in the descriptive passage contributes to the distastefulness it describes. More important than the static quality or mere boredom, however, is the aura of threat, the ominous, deadly pall which hangs over the entire proceeding.

The narrative voice of this story is split. The tale begins in a voice which could well be that of Morris himself, explaining that the following piece was prompted by a reading of Thorpe's *Northern Mythology*—an influential compilation of Scandinavian myths and folktales Morris had recently read. Then there is a spaced break in the story, and the narrative resumes in what seems to be a different voice: this time it is a priest who has been called to perform last rites for a dying man. The priest has been led into a trap by devilish unbelievers who have brought him there merely to make a mockery of all religious belief. He is surrounded by a decadent throng, "thrusting their horribly-grinning unsexed faces toward me till I felt their hot breath." This so repulses the narrator that he wants to quit the entire human race, "among whom, as it seemed, all sacredest things even were made a mock of."

The narrator escapes, and the horrid castle is transformed, hissing and gurgling, into the deep black lake known as Lindenborg Pool. Like the many changes of the first story, the final transformation here is into water—but the horrid aspect of Lindenborg Pool and its unalterable vegetation is seen only when set against the realization that the nature of water is movement and flux. This pool, composed as it is of the most mocking, complacently decadent representatives of the human race, is deadly and unmoving. At the end of the tale, this metamorphosis of evil has been accomplished through the prayers of a priest, who "knelt on the dear green turf outside, and thanked God with streaming eyes [note the image of water in flux associated with the good man] for my deliverance, praying Him forgiveness of my unwilling share in that night's mockery."

Here is an affirmation by the young and idealistic Morris that though he has changed his mind about a career in the church, he is far from abandoning deep conviction in the reality of "sacredest things." The "dear green turf" is an affirmation of the earth itself, and of a fruitful natural growth. In these stories one of the most common images of good or sacred things, also linked to the earth itself, is water—the natural, vital, changing symbol of transformation, and of transformation accomplished without great labor. Faith seems sufficient to affect change. The central characters are often passive witnesses of wonders which unfold beyond them, of powers and forces which shape the destiny and behavior of men. The narrator of this tale, while he has confronted a hideous mockery—an image of perversion as strong as anything Morris ever wrote—recognizes that the dimensions of the problem are greater than he has been able to imagine. "And this is how I tried to fathom the Lindenborg Pool," he tells us in the last line of the story. The suggestion is that this is only a partial attempt—the pool has yet to be fathomed. Human imagination clearly has limits in these stories, and the shape of human transcendence is recognizably framed within religious traditions.

A DREAM

"The Unknown Church" and "Lindenborg Pool" have, as Morris's earliest important biographer J. W. Mackail points out, a "semi-historical setting; they are placed, that is, in a definite European country and in a more or less definite epoch." The other five stories, however, move into a realm of pure fantasy. "The world of fantasy in which they are set is like and yet unlike that of the second cycle of prose tales which began more than thirty years later," Mackail observes, and although he does not greatly elaborate on this observation, it is an accurate way of directing our attention to the fact that Morris rapidly evolves beyond the purely conventional limits in the reality he depicts. "A Dream" freely associates narrative sequences, fantastical, non-realistic plot, and a dimension of evil which has a compelling attraction and control. Without the historical setting and familiar religious trappings, the tale is linked to reality almost exclusively by the dream device itself.

Two young lovers, Ella and Lawrence, quarrel. Ella asks Lawrence to demonstrate his absolute love for her by spending the night in the evil "cavern of the red pike," a cave in a cliff of red sandstone symbolically "between the green-growing grass and the green-flowing river." There are striking sexual suggestions in the phallic pike and the womb-like cave, and the red color of blood and passion which lends its color to this arbitrary and unreasonable test. The fixed and mysterious cave in the earth—both womb and tomb—is to become a significant and recurring symbol in the later fantasy novels. Here the lovers disappear into its depth.

The story is constructed once again like a nest of Chinese boxes: a dream about a group of men around a campfire telling stories about dreams and visions. It is involuted, idle story-telling. Lawrence, subject of one story, is essentially a passive hero, whose greatest "challenge" is to be still for one night inside a dark cave—surely an irrelevant way to prove one's love. In the various narratives, stillness is echoed in patterns of ominousness. A plague occurs because of a stillness in the wind; time does not move ("though the sun was high, I cast no shadow"); and the appearance of the lovers testifies that conventional visible time does not exist for them ("they were somewhat shy of each other after their parting of a hundred years"). Within the atmosphere of timelessness, all objects of reality assume an eternal, symbolic quality, particularly lilies and roses, a quality similar to the symbolism of Rossetti in his early paintings, or to the images in surrealist paintings.

Caught within the cave, the lovers are doomed to ghostly encounters, driven by a will of evil far greater than their own, though introduced by their own rather foolish and idle behavior. They are destroyed in the end by the same irreversible, inevitable, and personally passive fashion: "And as they gazed the bells of the church began to ring, for it was New-Years'-Eve; and still they clung together, and the bells rang on, and the old year died. And there beneath the eyes of those four men the lovers slowly faded away into a heap of snow-white ashes. The story is carved on the cold and silent marble of the tomb, but the associations this time aren't nearly so positive as those in "The Unknown Church." Here we begin to feel that if art has replaced religion, storytelling has merely replaced the tomb; art as tomb is merely the container of dead and idle matter—mere ashes. Not only are the lovers passive, helpless victims, but the dreamer-narrator is in a passive, helpless state, and the four story-tellers in his dream are equally helpless as the fragments of the larger tale fall together far beyond their individual or collective control. They watch, wait, and repeat, and when the tale is told, the sleeper awakes; reality is unaltered. The idle singer is carried here to extremes, and the influence of Poe can be discerned in the story's dark, destructive side. Morris soon overcame this death-obsessed exploration of the unknown side of human imagination, and the differences between Poe and Morris are evident in both artistic and autobiographical terms.

GERTHA'S LOVERS

"Gertha's Lovers," the longest of the early tales, gives evidence of nordic influences in both the names of the characters and the style of narration. While the characters are more active than those in "A Dream," the fabric of fate which controls the patterns of the action suggests that although individual deeds of great courage may be accomplished, the individual, is still essentially the passive pawn of a controlling destiny. The point is stressed in various ways throughout the story, from the chance meeting of Gertha, Leuchnar, and Olaf, through the accident of Borrace's death and the internal clash of horsemen against archers, to the mysterious death of Gertha herself.

Like "A Dream," the story tells of the results of love, this time a triangle reminiscent of Arthur, Lancelot, and Guenevere; it is also displaced in time and setting, more definitely than the earlier story: "Long ago there was a land, never mind where or when," Morris tells us in the first sentence. And, finally, like "A Dream," the tale is death-obsessed, closely associating love and death, and portraying a church built upon love's tomb, just as in "The Unknown Church" and "A Dream."

Divided into five chapers (and originally published serially in two issues of the magazine), "Gertha's Lovers" repays careful reading and thought. It explores "Goodness" in a complex and perceptive manner, creating King Olaf, Leuchnar, and Gertha as three saint-like heroes, leaders of a people at once devout and heroic: "Almost every man of that nation was a hero and a fit companion for the angels." The ideal of goodness is preserved to the end of the story, though the ideal is purchased only with the deaths of all the central characters. Morris's prose style seems to respond to the idealism he depicts, at once spare and lyrical, active and descriptive. King Olaf is first seen as "so beautiful, that he moved like the moving of music." As in the other stories, the movement—images of flux and change—is seen to be desirable. The people themselves are enacting a cycle: "They had a mighty faith withal that they should one day ring the world, going westward ever til they reached their old home in the east," and the warriors are referred to as "Sons of the men that go from east to west, and round again to the east!" King Olaf, associated with music as an image of his beauty, also is first seen singing softly to himself an old song. The verse of the song which Morris has both Gertha and Olaf sing is itself a kind of cycle of history repeating itself: "The King rode out in the morning early,/Went riding to hunting over the grass;/Ere the dew fell again which was then round and pearly,/O me—what a sorrow had come to pass."

11

Both King Olaf and Leuchnar fall in love with Gertha upon first seeing her while out hunting with a group of knights. Though they cannot speak to one another of the matter, each man knows that the other loves Gertha, and each resolves to sacrifice his own happiness in order to permit the desires of the other to be fulfilled. The largest portion of the tale is devoted to description of a bloody struggle in which the friends are fighting together on the same side for good cause. King Olaf is killed first, leaving a note with Leuchnar that Gertha is to become Queen and rule in his stead until the battle has been won. Olaf's death is described with the repeated use of cyclical and musical images, since they bury him in "a place *ringed* about with aspen-trees," and "tearlessly and sternly they watched the incense smoke rising white in the moonlight, they listened to the chaunting, they lifted up their voices, and very musically their sorrow was spoken." This first section, the first three chapters, appeared in the sixth issue (July 1856) of the magazine.

The tale was concluded in August, with Gertha becoming Queen and ruling until the enemy is defeated. In the fight, Leuchnar is killed, as well as Sir Richard and the other leaders who have fallen equally under Gertha's spell, who have become—as all the people become—"Gertha's lovers." After passing a just and forgiving sentence on the defeated army, Gertha delivers a farewell speech to her people, taking leave of them because it "is best both for you and me. If I were Queen much longer you would be disappointed in me, yet you would not say so, because you love me." She walks out onto the battlefield and enters the "circle of aspens" where Olaf is buried. Thereby she completes the circle as "there seemed to be silence over all the earth, except when she first stepped among the shadows of the trees, a faint breeze rose out of the south, and the lightly-hung leaves shivered, the golden haze trembled." Her handmaid is left to tell that she saw Gertha meet King Olaf in the meadow, that they joined hands and talked together, but that when she went to interrupt her mistress, she found her there alone, "lying dead upon the flowers, with her hands crossed over her breast, and a soft wind that came from the palce where the sun had set shook the aspen-leaves."

Death is depicted in terms of beauty despite inevitability. Heroism seems directly associated with death, and the people build a church on the spot "In memory of Olaf's deeds and Gertha's love"; Morris adds; "It was strange that this Church, though the people wrought at it with such zeal and love, was never finished: something told them to stop. . . and to this day the mighty fragment, still unfinished, towering so high above the city roofs toward the sky, seems like a mountain cliff that went a-wandering once, and by earnest longing of the lowlanders was stayed among the poplar trees for ever." These concluding images of incompletion are linked to eternity, and the rings and circles of the story nicely complement and prefigure the conclusion, in that they have neither beginning nor end in a clear sense. Like Gertha's resignation in the middle of her reign, there is an eternal and enduring aspect of the structure *in process* similar to the active version of Abraham in "The Unknown Church," an aspect which Morris finds far more compelling than the fully-wrought tombs in the earlier tales.

SVEND AND HIS BRETHREN

By contrast to the long story of "Gertha," "Svend and His Brethren" is a clean and fast-paced narrative. King Valdemar rules over a magnificent empire, what Morris was later to term "magnificent organization for the misery of life." The empire, like that of England or of Rome, extends its borders far afield, a conquest which contains the seeds of its own destruction. First, the policies of the king bend the land toward disintegration: "They drained the lakes, that the land might yield more and more, as year by year the serfs, driven like cattle, but worse fed, worse housed, died slowly, scarce knowing that they had souls." The nation is highly accomplished in engineering and technology—and in sophistry, for "their wise men could prove to you that any truth was false, till your head grew dizzy, and your heart sick, and you almost doubted if there were a God." The revolutionary movement in the land of the tyrant king is introduced in the present tense, in a condensed prose style based on fact and allowing no room for sophistry: "A walled town in the free land; in that town, a house built of rough, splintery stones; and in a great low-browed room of that house, a grey-haired man pacing to and fro impatiently: 'Will she never come?' he says. . . ." The effect of the shift is to cause the reader to identify more strongly with this alternative set of characters in active, present time.

The events then begin to pile up rapidly, and they are remarkably compressed. The plot line is enough to sustain a full-length fantasy—certainly one as long as "Gertha's Lovers"—but Morris tells it in about 7,000 words ("Gertha" is almost three times that long). The walled town, last citadel of the "good" people, has been cursed because once in battle long ago its soldiers set fire to a church wherein women were praying; the town has suffered ever since, but prophecy says that in the end the people will be saved by a woman. The old man's first words, "Will she ever come?", take on a wider significance when considered in light of the prophecy. The prediction, in fact, is fulfilled in the old man's own daughter, who returns, having just met the evil King Valdemar (whose name suggests, perhaps, that he is one who "mars" forests) who has offered to wed her. Cisella determines to sacrifice herself for the good of the decent folks who remain. She marries the king and mothers seven sons, of whom the most prominent is Svend. Cisella's old lover, Siur, becomes acquainted with the sons and forges armor and weapons for them. In conversations he encourages and awakens their ideals; visiting the smithy, Svend dreams of "restored nations" with himself as "the justest king in all the earth."

The tale ends in a frenzy of death. Siur, and Cisella are never united; they have sacrified their love, energy, and happiness for the good of the people. Cisella dies, then Valdemar dies of grief leaning upon her marble tomb, and the people riot in the street, refusing to follow the reforming sensibilities of Svend and his brothers. They draw the swords forged for them by Siur, and with their blades gleaming with the golden word "WESTWARD," the brothers lead all those who would follow them onto ten ships, leaving the people to themselves: "The streets ran with blood, and the air was filled with groans and curses."

A postscript supposedly written by another chronicler unveils the last vision of death. Good knights from the land of "Svend the Wonderful King" visit the old port years later. "So when they landed they found that which is hardly to be believed, but which is nevertheless true: for about the streets lay many people dead, or stood, but quite without motion, and they were all white or about the colour of new-hewn freestone, yet were they not statues but real men, for they had, some of them, ghastly wounds which showed their entrails, and the structure of their flesh, and veins, and bones. Moreover the streets were red and wet with blood, and the harbour waves were red with it, because it dripped in great drops slowly from the quays."

This is an image of final judgement which completes and extends the death-throes of the earlier tales. The men who could not reform their empire when the time and leadership arrived are turned to stone; their lack of motion is the physical embodiment of the static and inflexible attitudes Morris consistently deplores, and the vivid blood and entrails only make more apparent the contrast between their natural human nature and the rigid postures they are cursed to bear forever. The story reveals Morris increasingly distrustful of the British Empire, suggesting that great sacrifice and death will be required to turn things around. When the leadership does arrive, the citizens must have the imaginative flexibility and vision to go with the change, or face a horrible alternative. Moreover, he moves fully into a transhistorical perspective—one of the key aspects of his fantasy and utopian vision. The world and the characters in it cannot be viewed merely from the limits of individual perspective. The past, its misdeeds and its prophecies, shapes and guides the present, which in turn is shaping and determining the future. Morris's characters are willing to alter the course of their own lives for a cause far greater than themselves because they recognize (in this case through a dream-vision) the truth of the transhistorical forces. The narrators of the tale, possessing as they do an even greater perspective than the characters, pass the problems and questions along to the reader. Any reader truly responsive to Morris is bound to feel responsibility shift his way. What kind of judgment will the future make of us? Will our history be that of a frozen monument in time, or will we be a living part of the future? Morris constantly challenges us to broaden our perspectives. Progressively in his writing he was broadening his own.

THE HOLLOW LAND

The opening paragraphs of "The Hollow Land," to me the most haunting of Morris's early stories, nearly continue the desperate confusion of the downfall of Valdemar's kingdom: "Yea, in my ears in a confused noise of trumpet-blasts singing over desolate moors, in my ears and eyes a clashing and clanging of horse-hoofs, a ringing and glittering of steel; drawn-back lips, set teeth, shouts, shrieks, and curses." The narrator laments the "Lives past in turmoil, in making one another unhappy," but the narrative suddenly shifts tone and direction; the speaker introduces himself as Florian of the house of the Lilies, and begins to tell of the conflict between his house and that of Red Harald. Though the events are told by a single person, history and memory are confused and filled with contrasts which are particularly reflected in the shifting images of the first few pages.

The story is carefully structured, lending a formal order to the initial disorganized impressions; there are three chapters, the third of which is itself subdivided into three parts. The first chapter, "Struggling in the World," depicts the arbitrary cruelty of which powerful rulers are capable. In this case it is the Queen Swanhilda. Shown to be lusty, selfish, and murdering, she is slain by Florian of the lilies. The murder is carried out under the cover of religion, the murderers disguising themselves in white priests' robes to sneak up the white walls without being detected. The church is portrayed as a matter of convenient costume, rather than as an institution of significant social, moral, or political action. The evil Queen, murdered by these men in priests' clothing, is ultimately beyond the control of the established church and can be eliminated only by other individuals.

Section two is titled "Failing in the World," and reveals the consequences of deception and revenge, even if carried out for ostensibly good purposes, as in the case of the Queen's murder. The brothers find themselves suddenly entering a no-man's land, a moor country called "Goliah's Land," which belongs neither to their kingdom nor to their enemy Red Harald. The purity of the house of the lily is called into question in this "demilitarized zone"; here the clear

14

dichotomies of image (black/white) and morality (good/evil) are not clearly defined: "In the old time, before we went to the good town, this moor had been the mustering place of our people, and our house had done deeds enough of blood and horror to turn our white lilies red, and our blue cross to a fiery one." The overly simplified morality of the first section is explicitly questioned in Florian's narration when he asks, "Had our house been the devil's servants all along? I thought we were god's servants." Illusionistic aspects of religion, foreshadowed in the masquerade in the first section, are compounded by Florian's own men, as one knight alleges, "men say that at your christening some friend took on him the likeness of a priest and strove to baptize you in the Devil's name." With the familiar simplified perspectives gone, and the knights in a vulnerable position, about to be overtaken by Red Harald's forces, all is in doubt: "How would you feel inclined to fight if you thought everything about you was mere glamour; this earth here, the rocks, the sun, the sky? I do not know where I am for certain, I do not know that it is not midnight instead of undern: I do not know if I have been fighting men or only *simulacra*." Florian resists the doubts infecting the other knights, but cannot remain untouched when his brother Arnald, overcome by the same uncertainty and realizing his own death is approaching, repents his deceptive slaying of Swanhilda: "Now I know that it was a poor cowardly piece of revenge, instead of a brave act of justice." The incident represents in fictional terms the questions Morris had to ask himself regarding the revolutionary reformation of society. Even at this point in his life, he clearly saw injustice, and must have been prompted to strike out at it to revenge the victims; nonetheless, the "mere glamour" and *"simulacra"* caused him to doubt supposed realities in the external world, and to concentrate on the more manageable materials of his literary and visual arts. Florian sets aside Arnald's misgivings with a show of confidence, shrugging off impending destruction: "What harm brother?. . .this is only failing in the world; what if we had not failed, in a little while it would have made no difference. . . ." But for Morris, with his deep love of the earth, failing in the world increasingly came to represent failing altogether.

Florian, in battle with Red Harald, is driven backward into a crevice, and loses consciousness as he falls. He awakens in Chapter III, "Leaving the World," to gaze upon a woman, familiar and strange, at once a figure he recognizes as his Love, and "so lovely and tender to look at, and so kind, yet withal no one, man or woman had ever frightened me half so much." In clumsily trying to take his leave of her to search for his brother, Florian's sword sheath scrapes her hand and starts it bleeding. Immediately thereafter something causes a blood vessel in his own throat to burst, "and we stood there with the blood running from us on to the grass and summer flowers." It is a hauntingly archetypal scene, inexplicable, and yet highly significant. This is the Hollow Land beyond the world where the flowing blood which images life, vitality, and sacrifice upon the real earth here becomes an accidental, almost irrelevant event. The woman is symbolic of both love and fear, for she is an image of death, an attractive physical force in a world beyond physical reality; her very loveliness is fearsome because it is hollow. Having said this much, the complex layers of significance in the encounter still remain untouched. The scene must be associated with archetypes of myth and ritual which link it to passion and to sacrifice; and it seems to contain overtones of the Freudian sexually inspired death-wish.

Florian finally leaves this hypnotic lady to discover his brother, dead beneath a tree. Waiting by his brother's side, wailing, Florian is joined by the lady, who tells him she has been expecting him "all these years," that she has known he was coming ever since she was born: "As I grew up, I used to watch every

15

breath of wind through the beech-boughs, every turn of the silver poplar leaves, thinking it might be you or some news of you." Like the two-sided poplar leaf which represents light and dark, the two sides of the tree of life, the woman in this hollow land signifies the other side of reality. The episode ends abruptly. Florian's ritual wailing at his brother's end is, like the shedding of blood, mere show and "glamour" in this place. They bury Arnald among the roots of a beech tree (a tree of trust) and with this last link to his own blood-kin disposed of, Florian learns the lady's name is Margaret. As they are walking alone together, with the man believing they are the only two inhabitants of this strange new world, they suddenly spy a woman dressed in scarlet and gold. Margaret says, "Florian, I am afraid: let us come away." What Morris calls "Fytte the First" ("fytte," related to the icelandic "fitja" and Old English "fitt" or "fytte," is a term used to designate a part or section or a poem or song, or a canto; and has further meanings of conflict (fight), hardship or danger, or a fit of insanity) ends abruptly.

In the second "Fytte" Florian awakes in a mist to find he has grown old. He reaches to the top of his head and touches "a lump of slimy earth with worms coiled up in it." He flings away the slime and draws his sword, the only thing about him which has remained untarnished, and cheered somewhat by its gleam, he resheaths it and begins to run, stumbling over trees and brush, "so that my blood dropped on the dead leaves as I went." Suddenly he hears water, gives a leap, and finds himself in a black river about to drown. Near him is a boat with a man in it, and he swims towards it, but again he feels about to sink, unable to survive when the man (who is dressed in scarlet, like so many of the threatening figures of the story) spears him through the shoulder; Florian loses consciousness. He awakens on the bank of the river, naked, and recognizes his old family castle in the distance. Here is a familiar image from his past, and he sets out toward it, intending to die there. The castle is crumbling and he enters the decaying hall to find the walls covered with weird paintings in scarlet and yellow, of Red Harald, Swanhilda, Arnald, himself, and a beautiful woman he does not recognize. Finally he comes upon the painter, clothed in red and yellow, and it is the man in the boat, a man who says that he paints "God's judgments."

An argument ensues, the two men fight a very bloody battle, and Florian wounds the man. Afterward, however, he is sorry for the murder and slowly nurses the painter back to health. When he has recovered, the man teaches Florian painting; one day, as they watch the funeral procession of a great king Florian is moved to follow it, for he senses that it leads to the Hollow Land. Suddenly he calls the painter by his right name, Harald, and urges him to come but Florian can enter the Hollow Land only by himself, and the two men part as friends. Florian lowers himself carefully into the hollow and there falls asleep as "Fytte the Second" ends.

The story is the most abstractly symbolic of the early tales, and departs most dramatically from the traditional quest motif, entering the world of surrealism. The heightened, distorted, symbolic quality of the writing, and even the use of red and gold as images, suggest again the early paintings of Rossetti. While it is difficult to unravel a complete interpretation of the tale, several consistent concerns of the other stories recur here. The preoccupation with death and sacrifice (the conclusion may occur in an afterlife, with the central characters meeting in a Limbo) receives a psychological/sexual extension; matters of religion and "God's judgment" are equated with illusion. Events swallow the central character as he moves through a pre-ordained pattern, unable to shape and determine events for himself. Perhaps most significantly and uniquely, the central

16

character is out of touch with other real people, increasingly involved in enacting his own ideas about good and evil in a solipsistic reality which eventually results in his complete isolation.

"The Hollow Land" can quite well be read on one level as a mental aberration; certainly the surrealism in both symbol and action and the repeated shifts from waking to sleeping states contribute to this possibility. Florian is so much locked inside his own head that he is unable to distinguish between dream and reality (or ultimately between life and death). In the important conversation of chapter two, when Florian calls his fellow knight his "brother," he simultaneously denies this brotherhood by belittling the importance of what they do, "*only* failing in the world." He is detached from his fellows because he is detached from the world. At the end of the story, when Margaret and Florian approach the palace of art in the short "Fyte the Third," we can see dramatically revealed the attraction the youthful Morris felt for the detached, purely aesthetic and irrevelant realm of art. But we see too, with Morris, that it may well be an illusionistic reality, that Margaret's loveliness and love may be an artistic figment of a diseased imagination, from a frightened brain which has discovered itself touched by slime and worms. The beautiful final scene, and the haunting song, have only selfish attraction; politically and socially they are, like religion, hollow.

GOLDEN WINGS

"Golden Wings" couples isolation with even more extraordinary violence. If "The Hollow Land" deals with art-for-art's-sake as a central thematic issue, "Golden Wings" deals wih murder-for-murder's-sake. The first-person narrator tells how his mother would shut herself up in a tightly shuttered house each St. Peter's Day, and would sing a strange song and work at her sewing frame, telling her son to guard the door and let no man into the house. On the particular St. Peter's Day described, the narrator, suffering from the "shut-up heat," falls asleep and dreams a "foolish dream," which indeed is very foolish, especially compared to the more significantly symbolic dreams Morris has shown himself capable of inventing. He awakens from this nap to confront an armed knight who has broken down the door, killing the family dog. Lionel promptly slays the knight, for no particularly good reason, except that "I heard my mother's low mysterious song behind me, and knew not what harm might happen to her and me, if that knight's coming made her cease in it." After the murder, the mother finally comes to see her son, kisses him, and tells him he will be a king, "if the people will but know it." They bury the knight, and Lionel, inflated with self-importance at the prospect of being king, arms himself in a special armor his mother has buried, which carries the crest of two golden wings on a blue ground. As soon as he is armed, his mother lies down and dies. Lionel, the napping and unsung hero, mounts the dead knight's horse, and rides off to seek his fame

Lionel's isolation from the world of men is clear from the first sentence of the story, when he tells us that he never saw his father, and that his mother brought him up "quaintly." His first action as a "hero" is a barely conscious violent and unjustified murder. He attempts to join the court, but is not accepted. When he hears of an evil knight, he sets out to slay him alone, in order to gain all the credit for himself, but he is unsuccessful and nearly dies. He is saved by a noble knight whom Lionel decides is an enemy, and Lionel repays the favor by persisting in the wooing of that knight's fair-won maiden (though to give Lionel his due, the maid Alys does lead him on). Alys and Lionel are wed, but Sir Guy (who had won the maiden's hand in fair combat against Lionel) pursues Lionel and eventually overpowers him, though not before Lionel has lashed out viciously: "I turned and caught him by the ribs with my left hand, and with my right, by sheer strength, I tore off his helm and part of his nose with it, and then swinging him round about, dashed his brains out against the castle walls."

The tale concludes with Lionel kissing his fair Alys one last passionate kiss, and then, as Alys watches, "one thrust me through the breast with a spear, and another with his sword, which was three inches broad, gave me a stroke across the thighs that hit to the bones; and as I fell forward one cleft me to the teeth with his axe." The final one-sentence paragraph of the story reads simply, "And then I heard my darling shriek." It is a strange and horrifying conclusion. The violence is described in painstaking detail, and is particularly disturbing since the narrator is describing his own death. Yet, this is only the most dramatic example of something that has happened again and again in the early tales. Morris's heroes speak from beyond the grave to describe their dying. The detached way they are able to speak of what is happening to their own bodies is mirrored in their detachment in inflicting violence on others. The effect is to reduce the significance of the physical body, and to neutralize the effect of violent action by the very matter-of-fact way in which it is recounted. Life and death seem to be matters of relatively small consequence, especially when viewed from within the psyche of a single character. The ups and downs of life, even at its most extreme, seem arbitrarily determined by forces far larger than the individual—blind fate, perhaps—and forces not particularly concerned with the triumph of good over evil, or with the exacting of justice in a relatively meaningless universe. The point of view is almost existential, like that of Camus's narrator in *The Stranger*, curiously unmoved by a death he is expected to feel deeply.

Between the meaningless violence and existential isolation of the early stories and the next great period of Morris's prose fiction lies a time of deep social and artistic commitment. Thirty years later, in his next major work of fiction, Morris writes the utopian *Dream of John Ball*, in which the historical and revolutionary preacher serves as a vehicle for clarifying social and political ideals. The dream of a new human order allows Morris to connect personal significance with violent battle in a way which enhances the stature and importance of individualism and brotherhood, rather than leaving us with the hollow echo of an isolated shriek.

2. THE DREAM OF A BETTER WORLD

History and politics are largely missing from the short stories Morris published in his college days, though the tales clearly reach for visions beyond the ordinary, and show a transcendent dimension to reality with greater capacities for both love and terror. In his later writing, Morris becomes more specific in both political and historical terms, delineating his ideals, and contributing his hopes and dreams of a better world to the perennial search for social justice. In *A Dream of John Ball*, we are aware even from the title that this is an imaginary reality; Morris seems to feel the traditional dream-vision a necessary and logical excuse to take him from everyday life to an imagined history.

The narrative stance is masterfully chosen to allow Morris to reveal his own personality while setting the scene and leading the reader back in time. In a firm and straight-from-the-shoulder prose style, he gives us shreds of autobiographical material, including his architectural interest, and the first part of a dream in which he sees himself delivering a public address in his nightshirt while "the earnest faces of my audience—who would *not* notice it [the night-

18

shirt] . . . were preparing terribly anti-Socialist posers for me." Morris had begun to make regular socialist speeches in 1883, delivering eleven in the course of the year. From then until the writing of *John Ball* the number rose sharply, until his public lectures kept him constantly on the run: 52 in 1884; 67 in 1885; 90 in 1886; and more than 100 in 1887. The dream-vision, as his nightshirt lecture implies, must be seen in the context of the socialist message; Morris himself repeatedly delivered a message similar to the book's narrator, condemning the "degradation of the sordid utilitarianism that cares not and knows not of beauty and history."

Morris rejects "utilitarianism" because its overwhelming influence had been philosophically and politically degraded from the work of John Stuart Mill, and had been used to justify the social inequities and labor exploitation caused by the industrial revolution. Despite the clear links to his own personality and history, and his choice of an historical character from the English past, Morris displaces utilitarianism with fantasy. His historical imagination shows the England of the fourteenth century, when the radical preacher John Ball made his mark, to be a time not unlike his own. Locating his utopian impulses in a definite nationalistic past, Morris lends them credence and reality.

Utilitarianism, on the other hand, tended to reject many of the best lessons and characteristics of the past. Morris had condemned the habit in an 1884 lecture on the Gothic Revival, when he summed up his own day as a society "stripped of all art and poetry that is to say of all the pleasure of life: with history a despised desert behind us, with a blank prospect of mere utilitarianism before us." Mill's own political ideals in *On Liberty* were noble and fine, but the effects of utilitarian thinking (which reached its highest expression in Mill's *Logic*) narrowed the perception of human values which Morris set out to broaden again in *Ball* and his other lectures and writings. According to Mill, all truths not self-evident could be discovered only by inductions and interpretations of inductions. Morris's dream, by contrast, is a revelation of truth beyond the bounds of logic; part of the essential message of the dream is that the idea of history as progress is an inductive illusion. Morris shows his readers—through the noble sentiments of the fourteenth-century characters and the "garden-like neatness and trimness of everything"—that progress is a myth, the modern world a "degradation." Within the dream we are shown symbolic and self-evident truths which refute inductive absolutism.

In his dream, the narrator awakes, and the tale suggests through numerous paradoxes (e.g., that dreaming is awakening) that logical empiricism is not sufficient to feed man's highest needs. Particularly in the first portion of the tale, even the architecture speaks eloquently to dispell historical ethnocentrism: the village church, "which was large, and quite ravished my heart with its extreme beauty, elegance and fitness"; or the houses, with a "curious and invented carving about most of them" which seemed much more appealing than anything modern; and "though some were old and much worn, there was the same look of deftness and trimness, and even beauty, about every detail in them"; an ordinary pub is "so strange and beautiful. . . though it was but a pothouse parlour." He has recovered the truth accepted by Mill, but lost in the shuffle of commonplace Victorian interpretations of logical utility—the self-evident truth. The desirable aspects of life are self-evident if we will but look. And Morris confidently and convincingly begins with *John Ball* to present these truths to his readers through imaginary worlds where coherence and order can be figured forth as examples which seem tangibly right and meaningful, especially by contrast to the confused and complex misdirections of the real world.

19

Here, as in the earlier stories, religion figures prominently in the events. The first important architectural impression is of a church; the church bell summons the people to gather; their meeting takes place "at the cross" (crossroads, but the symbol is still there); and John Ball is a preacher. Morris has imagined that he himself is a travelling poet, "a tongue that can tell rhymes," and "my own master." The first man he meets, Will Green, decides, "thou comest from heaven down, and hast had a high place there too." Both Morris and Ball preach a radical religious message: "I say to you that earth and heaven are not two but one." The preacher asserts that "Fellowship is heaven" (a remark which may cast light upon the earlier observation that Morris came from Heaven); and he adds that "it is for him that is lonely or in prison to dream of fellowship, but for him that is of a fellowship to do and not to dream." The challenge "to do" is one which Morris himself had followed in both his artistic and political work, and the charge extends to the reader. The dream of fellowship is a simple and overwhelmingly appealing one: "Man shall help man, and the saints in heaven shall be glad, because men no more fear each other." The preacher mobilizes our best human intentions, and the men of Essex are moved to join with the men of Kent to fight the upper-class tyrants who would lord it over them. A battle follows, in which "the fellowship" is victorious over the establishment (knights, sheriff, and lawyers). Ball's victory speech urges the people on to London, a city which is the symbol of the economic and political power of the elite, in order that they themselves can symbolize in their presence the right cause of the common folk.

The focus of all the religious images is toward fellowship and commonwealth; this is a significant shift away from a religion concerned primarily with death, fear, and aesthetics. Chapter IX, a pivitol section where the various themes of the book come clearly into focus, takes place in "a goodly church and fair as you may see 'twixt Canterbury and London." The Chapter is titled "Betwixt the Living and the Dead," and deals not only with the matters of life and death for which Ball and his followers are fighting, but begins a dialogue between the living narrator and the dead Ball which continues from here to the book's end. The conversation provides insight into the past and its significance for the present, not in terms of progress or irrelevance, but in terms of fellowship and dialogue.

The narrator tells Ball, "Friend, I never saw a soul, save in the body." The fact that he is at that very moment commmunicating with the "soul" of Ball continues Morris's playful games with inductive reasoning and paradox; but more importantly the statement suggests that the intangible ideals and aspirations of the soul, if they are to be made manifest or real for either the present or the future, must be brought into physical existence. Anyone, therefore, who holds a religious belief in the existence of the soul must struggle to have it materialized in bodily form. As the narrator gazes with the preacher upon the bodies of the dead, each affirms the purposeful battle to bring about change; this fight cannot be dismissed as merely "failing in the world." The conversation in the church continues, with the poet Morris assuring the preacher that there will be a "change beyond the change"—a foreshadowing of the linguistic pattern he uses later in *The Wood Beyond the World*, and another wrench of utilitarian language. The narrator explains, "The time shall come, John Ball, when that dream of thine that this shall one day be, shall be a thing that men shall talk of soberly, and as a thing soon to come about."

In his biography of Morris, Jack Lindsay perceptively describes the concluding section of the book: "Here he brilliantly succeeds in re-creating this dream-method of his in terms of the new socialist world view. . . . John Ball

20

and Morris himself talk in the church, each man a dream-figment to the other, and yet, taken together, embodying a complete grasp of the essential forces in history. Morris's effort to explain to Ball what has happened to men in the five centuries following the Revolt, and Ball's effort to reach up out of the medieval categories of thought into the bourgeois situation, create a strange and powerful criss-crossing of ideas and reactions, which evoke richly the sense of what has happened to man and continues to happen and will continue, until all that is deepest in Ball's medieval sense of man and in Morris's struggle to re-create a sense of human wholes in the night of darkest alienation have united in a final assault on the citadels of division.''

This first work of book-length visionary fiction was, interestingly enough, published (like Morris's short stories) in a magazine he edited. He was made co-editor of the socialist monthly *Commonweal* in 1885, sharing the responsibility with Edward Aveling. In May, 1886, the paper became a weekly, with Morris as sole editor. This dream, and its re-creation of Ball's vision, was published serially there beginning in November, 1886. Ball's convictions gain added force when one realizes that Morris was working to embody his aims through the pages of *Commonweal*, in numerous lectures and meetings, and in the design work that he and his friends produced. He had written his school friend Cormell Price in 1856, "I can't enter into politico-social subjects with any interest, for on the whole I see that things are in a muddle, and I have no power or vocation to set them right in ever so little a degree. My work is the embodiment of dreams in one form or another. . . .'' While this has often been taken to indicate the idle and escapist side of his work, an interpretation which may be correctly applied to the 1856 stories, Morris himself shifted the stress from the *dream* to the *embodiment*: "Friend, I never saw a soul, save in the body.'' In shifting from the literary exercise of the collegiate *Oxford and Cambridge Magazine* to the politically purposeful *Commonweal*, and from the disturbing death-obsessed world of the early tales to the more purposeful deaths of *John Ball*, Morris has clearly moved to embody the dream, to make abundantly clear that a dream beyond the reach of mere utilitarian logic may well be worth the laying down of one's body.

THE HOUSE OF THE WOLFINGS

While writing *John Ball*, Morris had also been hard at work completing his translation of *The Odyssey*, which he published in 1887. Homer's mythic epic prefigures the great imaginative journeys of fiction, from *Tom Jones* and *Gulliver's Travels* to *Ulysses* and *2001: A Space Odyssey*. Morris admired it deeply, and intended his version to be "not a mere paraphrase of the original as *all* the others are. . . .I don't think the public will take to it; it is too like Homer.'' His English verions succeeds in countless ways, and Oscar Wilde said in his review in the *Pall Mall Gazette* that "Of all our English translations this is the most perfect and the most satisfying. It is, in no sense of the word, literary; it seems to deal immediately with life itself, and to take from the reality of things its own form and colour; it is always direct and simple, and at its best has something of the 'large utterance of the early gods'.'' The influence of Homeric techniques is not easily recognized in *John Ball*, but it is there in the determination "to deal immediately with life itself,'' and to deal with it in "direct and simple'' style.

There are stronger echoes to be found in *The House of the Wolfings*, where it serves as a model for the epic scope and the poetic aims of the book. The style in *Wolfings* is a further step into the distinctive "direct and simple'' approach

21

Morris had developed in the socialist lectures he began to deliver in 1883. May Morris explains in her introduction to Volume XIV of the *Collected Works*: "For some years now he had been forcing himself 'to say what he thought'—writing it mostly, indeed as he was for a long time no ready orator on a platform—but writing it in simple and forcible language that should get him into touch with his listeners as quickly and directly as might be. I doubt not that this self-discipline, the constant recitation of his thoughts—to put it that way—was one of the factors that went to develop his new narrative style." These qualities of simplicity and directness were traits Morris sought in his own life, and May Morris selects the *Odyssey* volume of the *Collected Works* to comment on Kelmscott House, Hammersmith, where the family moved in 1878. All of Morris's significant fantasy, from *John Ball* to *The Sundering Flood*, was written there; his long drawing room stood in drastic contrast to the stereotypical cluttered Victorian interior: "No picture, of course—the simple scheme of the room did not allow of such broken wall surface—no occasional tables, no chairs like feather-beds, no litter of any sort. Plenty of 'quarter-deck' in which to march up and down when discussions got animated and ideas needed exercise." This is the style, in life and language, from which *The House of the Wolfings* is constructed. Morris is in the habit of reflecting philosophy in the architecture of his fiction; and in the spare beauty of Kelmscott House, his final home, there is a statement very different from the one he made as a young college man, when he built the romantic Red House for his medieval bride. May Morris observes that "the man who once had built his Palace of Art as a refuge from inharmonious things without, will before long stand at Dod Street for Free Speech, and at the corner of mean roadways address a few careless listeners, in a growing, burning understanding of the difficulties of industrial life: from now until his strength failed, Art and Socialism cannot be spoken of apart."

Despite May's clear statement, Morris's fantasy writing is often read as pure escapist literature, with readers refusing to see the social and political significance in its construction. Reading the stories as political allegory would be foolish, as Morris himself pointed out to a simple-minded reviewer of his day. However, they should also not be viewed as his literary version of the Red House. With only a little reflection, one sees that far from being "a refuge from inharmonious things," these works directly portray a struggle or a fight capable of resolving the conflict present at the start of each story.

The Wolfings, like *The Odyssey*, has a vaguely historic setting, depicting, as May Morris tells us, "imaginary tribal life on the verge of Roman conquest—a period which had great fascination for the writer, who read with critical enjoyment the more important modern studies of it as they came out." Yet there is far less concern with nationalistic identity than with human identity. Adopting something of the voice of an epic bard, Morris announces boldly, "The Tale tells. . .," and the story itself is its own excuse for telling. There is no intermediary dreamer or dream to explain the imaginary vision.

Whether from Homer or from the natural growth of his own work, Morris has accepted directness as both a principle of candor and also as the most effective means of conveying the reality of his fictive vision. The language, still direct and forceful, is not questioned by being associated with a dream. In fact, Morris incorporates a conscious quaint or antique quality, employing archaic or linguistic root words, clear enough in their context, but casting an unfamiliar, special aura about the whole narrative. It is a way of achieving the heightened reality of dream-vision without allowing the dream to intrude as an explainable "excuse" for the events he describes. This unusual new voice of the *Wolfings*, in prose and verse, is a significant step into the unique voice of fantasy fiction. Like the world of fantasy, the voice is at once strange and familiar, epic and personal. Though the first paragraph begins, "The Tale tells. .," the third paragraph addresses the reader personally and directly: "You must know that this great clearing in the woodland was not a matter of haphazard." The setting is vastly distant in time and place; the narrator describes the strange in terms of the familiar. He explains, for instance, that the river is "about as wide as the Thames at Sheen when the flood-tide is at its highest." The narrator is obviously an Englishman, and one close enough to the terrain and geography of the English landscape to be aware of this detail; the reader is called upon to compare the distantly described and somewhat vague places and events to the country with which he ought to be best acquainted. While many critics, and not a few readers, find the language and narrative stance peculiar at first, the charm and magic of the extraordinary language work their spell with time. Morris set the direction for the fantasy genre in this as in so many aspects of his fiction, and the special language of fantasy survives in our own day in the work of Tolkien, Burgess, Vonnegut, and many others.

As we might expect form the title, the "hero" of the novel, in a departure from epic tradition, is the tribe, the "folk," the Wolfings, a group well into the Iron Age, but on the verge of Roman conquest. Here is the conflict of "inharmonious things" which the fantasy confronts rather than escapes. The tribe is introduced through detailed nature images, and as a folk they are more concerned with making their peace with nature than with quarrelling with their fellow men: "They stayed their travel, and spread from each side of the river, and fought with the wood and its wild things, that they might make to themselves a dwelling-place on the face of the earth." They diked and tamed the river, "and it became their friend, and they loved it, and gave it a name, and called it the Dusky, and the Glassy, and the Mirkwood-water."

The tribe is organized into "'houses' of men; for by that word had they called for generations those who dwelt together under one token of kinship." The explanation of vocabulary does, in fact, consume a good deal of the first chapter. In the process of defining some special terms (Thing, Mid-mark, Doom-ring, Thing-stead, etc.) Morris begins to create his convincing alternative world; it is only fitting that this different sort of reality should have special names for its distinctive features. He is able to provide a great deal of story information about the Folk of the Markmen while he explains and defines the new and unfamiliar words.

Among the special objects introduced, the most important is the wondrous glass lamp called the Hall-Sun, which "was held as an ancient and holy thing by all the Markmen, and the kindred of the Wolf had it in charge to keep a light burning in it day and night forever." They appointed an unwed woman to be in charge of it, and this fairest of women was called by the name Hall-Sun. The folk gather around a minstrel to hear tidings of approaching war. Beneath the Hall-Sun, surrounded by tapestries which tell the history of the folk so they are "amidst the woven stories of time past," they hear of the invaders who speak an unknown tongue and come from cities of the South—Roman armies that will sweep the less "civilized" Goths and Huns away before their disciplined legions. The folk must prepare for war, and they gather their armor and weapons in order to leave the next morning.

Thiodolf, wisest of the Wolfings, and father to Hall-Sun, sits alone in the great hall until all the folk are asleep, and then walks out into the moonlight, deep into a pathless wood, where he encounters the magical Wood-Sun: "There on a stone chair sat a woman exceeding fair, clad in glittering raiment, her hair

23

lying pale in the moonlight on the grey stone as the barley acres in the August night before the reaping-hook goes in amongst them." He embraces her, a daring act, for we find that she is a daughter of the gods, and Thiodolf sings a rhymed story of how she first appeared to him as a young man after his glorious fight against the Huns. Despite Thiodolf's bravery, he had been slain. In the epic tradition of Athena protecting Odysseus, the goddess Wood-Sun had restored Thiodolf to life and had been his lover and protector ever since. She warns him of the power of Doom, and tells him that, although she has stood by him in forty brave battles, a power larger than herself—Weird, or fate— has ordained that she may not go out to this upcoming fight. She has spied on the enemy, however, and tells Thiodolf that they are "the folk of the cities"; they live "mid confusion of heaped houses, dim and black as the face of hell." She has seen their battle-gear and acknowledges the "ordered wisdom of the war-array." She urges Thiodolf not to join this fight, not to sacrifice himself to a "fruitless death of the war-wise, and the doom of the hardy heart." She wants him to wear a magic armor of grey rings, made by the Dwarfs in the ancient days, which will assure the life of whoever wears it. Though Thiodolf is not content to violate the custom of his people, which holds that a hero should shed his armor at the end of an unsuccessful battle and die a hero's death rather than retreating or surrendering, he does leave the wood the next morning wearing the dwarf-wrought protection.

This initial encounter with the goddess is typical of the epic and romance conventions. In a study of pastoral elements in Morris's work, Blue Calhoun has made clear that within his landscapes there is often a "sacred precinct" in which the protagonist finds the awakening of new emotions, hints of new dimensions of reality from which he begins a new aspect of growth. There is, paradoxically, often an isolating factor associated with such experiences. One might think of these "sacred precincts" as akin to the land the lovers enter at the end of "The Hollow Land." The negative aspects of the sacred precinct in the *Wolfings* are found in "the hauberk's threat to tribal unity. Its protection to Thiodolf isolates him from death, a part of natural processes, and from the tribe and its natural activities. In sacrificing the hauberk, he breaks its spell of subjective isolation and literally reimmerses himself in human and natural process." More importantly, he reaffirms history, the past cultural and mythic traditions of his people, as well as his own upbringing within these values, rejecting the ahistorical realm of the goddess.

The tale of the struggle to preserve a primitive tribal community in the face of conquering Roman warriors is also a tale of the conflict between communal, pastoral existence (feminine in its cultivation of mother earth), and the urban, empire-building ideal of the male-dominated warrior culture of Rome—a representative struggle of country vs. city, handicraft vs. industrial exploitation, communism vs. totalitarianism. Roughly rooted in history, the action is centered at the foot of the Italian Alps, and the older epic traditions might have been more prominent if the story had been told from the Italian (Roman) perspective. We are bound to have something of this in mind as we read the story, for Morris has used history as the Greeks would use mythology. We know from the beginning what will happen: Rome will win and "civilization" will spread. We recognize further that Morris has chosen his side with the tribal culture, doomed to die at the hands of the Romans; the hero Thiodolf, who will lay down his life for his people, will represent the human cost of the loss the Romans are about to inflict.

John Hollow has written of the conflicts resolved in the late novels as examples of "Deliberate Happiness." In that discussion, Hollow points out that both

John Ball and Thiodolf are reformers on this imperfect earth. "Thiodolf's only choice," he writes, "is whether to live for himself or to die for his people. It is not the choice of Achilles (long life or fame), nor is his need that of Beowulf (who of all the Geats was the 'most yearning of fame'): when Thiodolf refuses to wear the dwarf-wrought hauberk, he chooses not so much the immortality of fame as the immortality of fellowship. If Thiodolf lives on, it is as a part of the life of his people." Hollow's beautifully presented view of Morris's assumptions concludes with reference to C. S. Lewis, a great admirer of Morris and a writer of fantasy himself: "C. S. Lewis said the center of Morris was not the contrast between an unearthly and an earthly paradise [the Palace of Art; the land at the end of 'the Hollow Land'], but a 'tension' between 'the passion for immortality' and 'the feeling that such desire is not wholly innocent, that the world of mortality is more thn enough for our allegiance." This is clearly the message of Thiodolf, as it is later of Hallblithe and Steelhead.

Hollow continues in his essay to observe that "Perhaps even closer to the truth is the suggestion that this tension is just one of the tensions, albeit an important one, in a poet whose lines are full of pairs such as 'joy and sorrow,' 'pleasure and pain,' 'hopes and fears' and 'life and death.' If Morris's prose romances have anything in common, it is this overwhelming awareness of contrasts, of change from one state to another, as the defining characteristic of both the life of mankind and the way of the world. The change and the contrasts may be subject to pattern, as in the seasons of the year, but for Morris contrast is the most real part of the pattern." These prose romances do indeed have a great deal in common, much of it related to the investigation of pattern and tension, an inquiry that may be seen as part of the operation of what was by nature a dialectical mind, perhaps one of the reasons a Marxist theory of history could intuitively make sense to him. The dialectical operation of thematic elements is evident, for instance, in the oppositions and unions of male and female protagonists.

A major shift which occurs in *Wolfings* is the first appearance in Morris's fiction of significant female characters. *John Ball* presents its idealistic social order primarily through the male perspective, but in *Wolfings* Morris devotes substantial attention to women. Thiodolf has survived his battle injuries only because of Wood-Sun; and Hall-Sun, daughter by their union, is entrusted with the most cherished symbol of the tribe. Both women are associated with transcendence: Wood-Sun foreknows that Thiodolf will be killed unless he wears the hauberk; Hall-Sun foresees that Thiodolf's tribe will perish in a vision of the House consumed by flames (it's interesting that this vision is immediately followed by a recognition scene, in which the Wood-Sun shows herself to Hall-Sun and allows her the knowledge that she is her mother).

Morris reveals these strong women as images of liberty opposed to the male-dominated Imperium of Rome. In one sense, the thematic dichotomy of freedom vs. slavery is imaged in the wolf. The Wolfings use the image of an unfettered animal close to nature, one which runs in packs and therefore symbolizes the natural community. The contrast to Roman civilization is obvious, for Morris points out the large number of slaves in the Roman camp: "Their thralls be not so well entreated as their draught-beasts." The animal image associated with the upper-class Romans is an even more negative one: "Above these are men whom they call masters and lords who do nought, nay not so much as smither their own edge-weapons, but linger out their days in their dwellings and out of their dwellings, lying about in the sun or the hall-cinders, like our cur-dogs who have fallen away from kind." By presenting thesis and antithesis, in action and image alike, Morris hopes to represent not annihilation, but synthesis.

Thiodolf's final actions affirm the synthesis, as the conflict of hero and lover is resolved by relinquishing both to the good of the community and its history. Thiodolf is a pagan Christ figure, but one stemming from the Mother Earth, rather than from a father-ruler on high. His tribe is agrarian and close to the soil, and his death will be merely a return to that soil. As Thiodolf begins to understand the mysterious power of the hauberk, he realizes that it will assure his existence only in terms of worldly temporality; at the same time it singles him out, isolating him from the very community which defines his purpose and identity. He is able to reject the protection of the dwarf garment because it will diminish his human stature. In so doing, he affirms the human faith and courage which identify him as a Wolfing. Like Christ, his identity at death is clarified in both human and transcendent terms. Thiodolf dies not in the service of divinity or personal glory, nor for the lady he loves, but in fulfilling courage and goodness beyond himself, his destiny as a member of the human community. His resurrection occurs in the end through his story, shared in a Wolfing song, retold by Morris: "All men's hearts rose high as he sang. . . for in sooth at that moment they saw Thiodolf, their champion, sitting among the gods. . . . "

THE ROOTS OF THE MOUNTAINS

One of the common elements of Morris's novels is the presence of landscape as symbol. His three most primitive and fundamental descriptive symbols are water, wood, and mountain (with its opposite, plain), and beginning with *The House of the Wolfings*, the symbols develop increasing complexity in *The Roots of the Mountains*, *The Glittering Plain*, *The Wood Beyond the World*, *The Well at the World's End*, *TheWater of the Wondrous Isles*, and *The Sundering Flood*. In the *Wolfings* the land is relatively flat: "Though as for hills you could scarce say that there were any," and yet the swiftness of the water seems to suggest the presence of mountains, "so swift and full of eddies, that it gave token of mountains not so far distant, though they were hidden."

The great Victorian essayist John Ruskin, an important influence on Morris's art and thought, was the most influential Victorian spokesman to point out the unique position of the mountain in nineteenth century art. He spent almost half of *Modern Painters* discussing the theme, which he found to be "no more explicable or definable than that feeling of love itself." He concluded that the symbol was associated with "love of liberty," presaging a change from the "Mountain Gloom" of older classical, medieval, and Renaissance art to the nineteenth-century recognition of "Mountain Glory." The contemporary critic Marjorie Hope Nicolson has extended and expanded Ruskin's views on the mountain, delineating changes of attitude toward the symbol in the writings of Romantic and Victorian authors as part of "the development of the aesthetics of the infinite." Morris works with the symbol in its overpowering and infinite sense, but insists that the infinite has its roots in the earth. This is touched upon in Nicolson's essay, when she points out that the new attitudes embody "a sacred theory of the earth." Morris makes that aspect particularly prominent in *The Roots of the Mountains*, a novel published just a year after the *Wolfings* in 1889.

Symbolically, thematically, stylistically, and historically the two books are closely related. He began the new work shortly after finishing *Wolfings*, mentioning in a letter to his daughter that there were some differences: "For one thing the conditions of the people I am telling of is later (whatever their date

26

may be) than that of the Wolfings. They are people living in a place near the Great Mountains.'' In the same letter, he indicates a stylistic shift: "This time I don't think I shall 'drop into poetry,' at least not systematically.'' The drop into poetry was at least partially associated with the earlier historic period in which *Wolfings* was set, but also it had about it a "systematic'' framework. Poetic style was appropriate to *Wolfings* because its regular cadences and vigorous rhythms suited the inevitable march of events which it depicted. The alteration of prose and poetry emphasized the special artistic and elevated quality of the language itself, and convincingly rendered in written form the precious gift of human speech so cherished by the Wolfings. In *Mountains*, the arrangement is more open. Sustained passages of poetry, requiring a tighter discipline and structure than the prose, would not properly represent a sense of possibility Morris hopes to convey.

Language and form are consistently used to reinforce symbol and theme in Morris's fantasy fiction. It is a principle of good design or pattern that correspondences and repeated motifs should make themselves felt in such a way that we recognize the unity of the design and the presence of the pattern, but not so much that the repeated elements overwhelm us by their repetition, distracting from our appreciation of the individual details. Frederick Kirchhoff charts the right path for a linguistic and stylistic analysis of Morris in his "Introduction'' to a recent publication by the American branch of the William Morris Society, *Studies in the Late Romances of William Morris*. Early reviewers, he says, "failed to grasp the genuinely radical nature of Morris's experimentation with language.'' the language is "radical'' in the sense that it drastically shakes up our current assumptions in language usage, and forces us back to our linguistic roots and origins. Kirchhoff correctly points out that "his extensive use of archaic terminology is not so much an attempt to evoke the past as it is to revitalize the language through a return to its Germanic roots. Just as the romances themselves oppose the 'healthy' world of the Germanic gens to the decadence of Rome, their diction deliberately substitutes a Germanic for a Latin vocabulary. No quaint self-indulgence, this vocabulary, coupled with the controlled simplicity of Morris's syntax, is inseparable from the ethos of the romances. For he is as much concerned with setting forth a way of thinking—or story-telling—as he is with the story line of the narration.''

In the early short stories, Morris's characters were driven by forces far beyond themselves, and often overwhelmed and defeated by those forces. In both *Wolfings* and *Roots*, we feel the sweep of historical forces, but they continue the direction of *John Ball* in showing that the individual character attains heroic stature by asserting his own terms and affirming his own meanings in the face of larger forces. The concept of hero is enlarged in the process, and if, as I have suggested, there is a Christ-like quality in the character of Thiodolf, this heroic dimension is even more evident in the name of the hero in *Roots*, Face of god. *Roots* is concerned with the "infinite'' aspects of the mountain symbol (God often appeared on the mountain top), but Morris brings this world beyond the world down closer to its roots in everyday life. Face-of-god is a character who shows us divinity in purely human form. In doing so, he calls to the best in each of us to reach toward the infinite potential within our grasp.

The House of the Face, like the House of the Wolfings, becomes a secular tribal "temple''; and Face-of-god is possessed by a longing for something indescribable, something beyond that familiar world he inhabits: "I fared as if I were seeking something, I know not what, that should fill up something lacking to me, I know not what.'' This sense of longing is inexplicable, what some analysts have termed "undifferentiated desire.'' It reflects the feeling most of us have when we yearn for something better than we know, for the fulfillment of a dream or the attainment of an impossible ideal. The idealism, which we first sense in adolescence and youth, is usually dwarfed by practical concerns by the time we reach adulthood, but what can be more *practical* than the need for a healthy and idealistic vision? Morris discovered a way of embodying that sense of idealism in a literature which would remind an adult audience of the necessity for imaginative leaps into the unknown.

Face-of-god does indeed feel satisfied temporarily to be among his own people. He has a loving father and a beautiful girlfriend (the Bride). His father, Iron-face, is sympathetic to his son's restless dissatisfaction, and urges him to visit the plains and the cities. In consistent geographical symbolism, the plain connotes everything that the mountain denies: it is flat, repetitive, unimaginative; it attains no heights. The city represents the tyranny of rational organization. Cities are citadels of economic power, where a wealthy elite rules at the expense of an enslaved working class. This, as far as anyone knows, is the way it always has been—but Face-of-god, like many of us, feels a sense of unease. There must be something better, and the answer will not be found in the city life, but at some complete alternative.

Morris uses the names of his characters to suggest abstract symbolic dimensions. Stone-face and Iron-face symbolically imply that the stone and iron ages—those crucial periods when technology gave men great power over nature and one another—have little to offer the youthful pilgrim Face-of-god, who is also called Gold-mane, and is idealistically in pursuit of a golden age. No eminent danger from outside threatens his existence. No fear of impending death or doom clouds the motivation. Morris asks us to recognize the desire we all feel for altered circumstances; and he asks us, in the example of his hero, to *act* upon that desire.

Face-of-god is drawn onto the road with no sure destination. "What road than farest thou away from us," asks a good wife. "The way of my will," Gold-mane replies. The impulse had been accounted for in different terms in Morris's earlier writing. The characters there were driven by Fate, or motivated by religion or concern for human well-being; this character is driven by an internal impulse. Morris suggests that his vision may be equally reached by internal or external motivation. Face-of-god enters the forest, a symbol of mystery and a common literary convention of religious allegory and popular fiction. The forest is a place of confusion, like Dante's dark wood in the *Inferno*, a place isolated from the sun, closer to Mother Earth than to Father Sun, closer to intuition or instinct than to rational power. In this feminine forest (similar to the realm where Thiodolf met Wood-Sun) Face-of-god finds the woman he calls the Friend, whose real name is Sun-beam.

The women of the novel are all guides to Face-of-god, serving this role in various capacities. In this respect, the mystical number three becomes prominent in the story pattern. The Bride, companion of his boyhood and a promise of union, fulfills the *anima* function until the need becomes more manly when the child grows into an adult. Then Boy-may plays a role akin to a female Cupid; she is associated with the phallic arrow, acting as go-between for Face-of-god and the Friend. Face-of-god, after proving himself in battle, accomplishes a fertile and masculine union with the female *anima* principle; there are three "preparatory" encounters prior to his full perception of her: his initial quest, which leads him to the pine-wood; his encounter with Bow-may during winter, when she leads him home again; and the sign of the token, which draws him to the Image of the Wolf and the Sun-beam. Face-of-god's third and most significant encounter with the Friend begins with a sexually suggestive scene in which the number three is conspicuous: "He smiled and took the spear from her, and poised it and shook it till it quivered again, then suddenly drew back his arm and cast, and the shaft sped whistling down the dim hall, and smote the aforesaid door-lintel and stuck there quivering: then he sprang down from the dais, and ran down the hall, and put forth his hand and pulled it forth from the wood, and was on the dais again in a trice, and cast again, and the second time set the spear in the same place, and then took his other spear from the board and cast it, and there stood the two staves in the wood side by side; then he went soberly down the hall and drew them both out of the wood and came back to her, while she stood watching him, her cheek flushed, her lips a little parted."

Face-of-god has been led to the primitive House of Desire where he must prove his masculinity and his right to possess the Friend. He earns the right to the shining maiden by vanquishing the dark forces of the Dusky Men. And beyond the connection of names [Thiodolf—Face-of-god; Hall-Sun/Wood-Sun= Sun-beam], the rugged mien of the image of the Wolf extends the historical symbology of the *Wolfings*. Here the image is clearly archetypal, carved upon rock by the mind of man: "The stone wherein the image was carved was darker than the other building stones, and might be called black; the jaws of the wood-beast were open and gaping." It is quite a different portal than the one faced by the characters in "The Hollow Land," and an unexpected but more mature path to the Sublime. Having passed these gates, the characters face each other as sexually mature adults. Sun-beam expresses herself directly: "O Goldmane, O speech-friend, if thou wert to pray me or command me that I lie in thine arms to-night, I should know not how to gainsay thee." And when they kiss, it is an embrace of equals: "And when their lips met, he felt that she kissed him as he her."

The joining of lovers is prelude to the restoration of a larger idealistic social order. Their marriage cannot be fulfilled until they set off toward home. Purified and refreshed by a morning bath, Face-of-god is prepared for his first battle where he and the others score a decisive victory over the Dusky Men. "I fight for the ceasing of war and trouble," Face-of-god explains. The goodness of his motives, and the light-dark imagery, reinforce the abstract clash of good and evil. This fundamental struggle is what actually must occur at the roots of the mountain: the battle must be won before they can ascend the slope. And only when this point in the narrative is reached does Morris elaborate the metaphor of the title: "They were going athwart all those great dykes that went from the ice-mountains toward the lower dales like the outspread finger of a hand or the roots of a great tree." The tree which immediately comes to mind is Yggdrasill, not simply because of Morris's interest in Northern mythology, but also because of related suggestions earlier in the book. Face-of-god's father, for instance, has the hammer as "the token of his craft and of his God." The hammer is a symbol closely linked to Thor; at Icelandic *Things* (court assemblies), Thor is the ancient god traditionally invoked in testimony of oaths. The wolf is prominent in Norse legend, particularly as the animal guardian of Odin. Face-of-god and his father are, in fact, roughly comparable to Thor and Odin; mythographer Joseph Campbell explains that "the god Thor retains in his character something of the crude dawn memories of his people—the paleolithic hammer and the bold works of the primitive giant-killer—in the character of Wodan (Othin, Odin), primitive traits have all but disappeared, giving place to a steely-bright symbolic figure, highly fashioned and of great surface brilliance, but also of astounding depth." Mythically the characters may be reversed—in Norse legend Thor was Odin's son—but Campbell dates him (Thor) as the oldest figure in the pantheon, going back possibly to the paleolithic (Stone age=Stone-face).

Face-of-god embodies several aspects of Christ, but mythically his nature is better conveyed in the Icelandic crucifixion. Campbell provides Bellows's translation of Odin's famous lines from the Icelandic poetic Edda:

> *I ween that I hung on the windy tree,*
> *Hung there for nights full nine;*
> *With the spear I was wounded, and offered I was*
> *To Othin, myself to myself.*
> *On the tree that none may ever know*
> *What root beneath it runs.*
>
> *None made me happy with loaf or horn,*
> *And there below I looked;*
> *I took up the runes, shrieking I took them,*
> *And forthwith back I fell.*
>
> *Then began I to thrive and wisdom to get,*
> *I grew and well I was;*
> *Each word led me on to another word,*
> *Each deed to another deed.*

Odin, like Christ, is the man/god, but clearly a more secular figure. Face-of god is in a sense wounded into knowledge through the pain of his own desire, symbolized by the spear and arrows. He interprets the "runes" of the wood-mysteries which were mistakenly read by Stone-face, Iron-face, and the other elders, to unite that which was divided or severed. He destroys his identity with his own kindred (sunders himself from himself) in order to join the Sun-beam and her people in their fight, at the same time giving himself to himself by uniting with the tribes in brotherhood and giving his own son to the Bride.

Face-of-god survives to marry and enlighten his people, a complete reversal of endings of every previous fantasy. Campbell's explanation of the unique aspects of Odin's crucifixion helps to clarify this change in focus: "All-father Othin hung upon the tree and, like Christ upon the cross, was pierced by a lance: the lance, his own; and he is a sacrifice to himself (his self to his Self) to win the wisdom of the runes. The analogy to be made, however, is rather to the Buddha at the Bodhi-tree than to Christ upon the cross, for the aim and achievement here was illumination [the Sun-beam], not the atonement of an offended god and the procurement thereby of grace to redeem a nature bound in sin. But on the other hand, in contrast to the Buddha, the character of this Man of the Tree is entirely *with* the world, and, specifically, in heroic-poetic disposition."

The book ends with general marriages, the highlight being the union of Gold-mane and Sun-beam. The tribes are also ritually married and agree to renew their covenant every three years, meeting in Shadowy Vale at the roots of the mountains. Gold-mane's second-born son is given to the Bride. The mood at the end of the book is one of peace and rest: "High floated the light clouds over the Dale; deep blue showed the distant fells below the ice-moun-tains; the waters dwindled." The tale is a clear statement of victory for the "heroic-poetic disposition," and the "deep blue" color, symbolic of imagina-tion, lends the scenery something of the character of the blue hills in "The

Hollow Land." The "sheer rocks" and "rocky heaths" of the opening paragraphs of this story give way to air, spaciousness, and height of vision in the final scene. As the American poet Wallace Stevens says in one of his poems:

In this plenty, the poem makes meanings of the rock,
Of such mixed motion and such imagery
That its barrenness becomes a thousand things.

NEWS FROM NOWHERE

American author Edward Bellamy published his socialist utopia *Looking Backward* in 1888, projecting an ideal future society built on a widely-expanded technology. The fact that Bellamy was, like Morris, a socialist, caused Morris to consider the work more seriously than he would have otherwise, for all of Bellamy's suggestions ran against the non-urban social vision which Morris held as an ideal. In reviewing the work in *Commonweal* in 1889, Morris admitted he was shocked to find Bellamy's imagination so limited that he conceived "of the change to socialism as taking place. . . by means of the final development of the great private monopolies. . . . He supposes that these must necessarily be transformed into one great monopoly which will include the whole people and be worked for the benefit of the people. . . . In short, a machine life is the best which Bellamy can imagine for us on all sides." Though Morris had clearly developed a social vision in opposition to Bellamy's in *John Ball*, *Wolfings*, and *Roots*, he evidently felt these were not explicit enough in their total utopian projections, and in 1890 began publishing his own utopia serially in *Commonweal*, with book publication in Boston (Bellamy's home turf!) later the same year.

News From Nowhere has been Morris's most consistently popular novel, widely read and discussed in English-speaking countries, and widely translated. Sales of a recent German paperback, for instance, have been good, showing that the vitality of the vision is undiminished. The utopia has been a part of English literature since Thomas More coined the term as the title of his ideal society in 1516, and *News From Nowhere* should be seen more within this tradition than as part of the English fantasy novel. However, it is important for our purposes to recognize the continuity of imagination and intellect; the same mind is present in both the fictive fantasies and in this appealing utopian novel. More plainly and directly than any other book, *News* allows us to see the consequences of the changes Morris advocates.

Similar in intent to *John Ball*, *News* is a far more ambitious work, not only in length, but in the precise application of utopian ideals. Extending and broadening the dream device, Morris uses this as a structural approach to the story, but also asserts that the dream can be altered from individual consciousness to collective reality when it is shared by others. The imaginative power which is capable of conceiving worlds beyond this world can be applied in practical terms to change the shape of human society. This is an obvious example of the truth in May Morris's remark that "art and Socialism cannot be spoken of apart" in her father's work.

News gives further evidence of Morris's concern with the question of time: where does the temporal reality of the book stand in relation to his own time? In each of the three novels we have examined, he has depicted *past* time, but in *News* the events are set in an unknown future where time lines become blurred and faint, much as in *Roots*; we have some vague sense of where we are, but the dating is never specific. The society is post-21st century, and in the seventeenth

31

chapter—nearly halfway through the book—we are told "How the Change Came" with revolution: "The year 1952 was one of the worst of these times; the workmen suffered dreadfully: the partial, inefficient government factories, which were terribly jobbed, all but broke down, and a vast part of the population had for the time being to be fed on undisguised 'charity' as it was called." By providing details of the events leading up to the revolution, and dating this connective material in real time, the fantasy is linked closely to known temporal reality. In doing so he elevates the utopianism of the book to social prophesy presented with conviction. "Basically, Morris viewed politics as a philosophical pursuit of happiness," Philip Henderson observes in his excellent biography, "and it is as visions of happiness and of a regenerated humanity that his later prose romances should be viewed."

Morris's use of time can be more clearly understood by comparison with a near contemporary, H. G. Wells. Although Wells was thirty-two years younger than Morris, he published *The Time Machine* in 1895, just five years after *News*. Like Morris, Wells was a social critic, and enjoyed combining this criticism with scientific speculation in novel format. The contemporary science fiction writer Samuel R. Delany has written that the emergence of science fiction in the nineteenth century was an understandable outgrowth of Victorianism: "Wells' 'Romances of the Future' come from much the same impulses that produced his monumental multivolume *An Outline of History*. The future stories were an outgrowth of the perfectly viable fancy that history might well continue beyond the present. Both the historical work and the SF, however, fell out of the same twin Victorian views: that man's knowledge, in general, and his technology, in particular, develop in a more or less orderly way; and also that, in any given situation, human behavior will always be more or less the same, no matter when, or where." Delany's description is particularly apt for Wells, and can perhaps be applied to most science fiction now being written; but it is not so applicable to Morris.

Time in Wells's science fiction stories is nearly always circular. Even though characters move through time, they are still part of it. *War of the Worlds* is the closest Wells comes to a true eschatologicl vision, and this too is part of a circle, war and the rumors of war, which man has been repeating endlessly since Zeus slew Typhon or Cain murdered Abel. Here we have a primary difference between English science fiction—founded by Mary Shelley and Wells—and the fantasy tradition stemming from Morris: science fiction is more "realistic" than fantasy in the sense that it sees time, history, and human nature as essentially repetitive. Evolution may alter the outer shapes and forms, but the inner structures and fundamental motivations and actions of societies and individuals will remain the same.

Fantasy makes a different assumption. It allows itself the imaginative freedom to redeem both human nature and society. There is the constant possibility of transformation, often unnoticed, because this is what we expect of magic. Scholar Mircea Eliade explains it as a different use of history, taking myths of an Edenic or Golden Age in the past, and projecting them into a timeless future. If the revelations of the past (unconscious mind) can be transformed through imaginative projection into future social reality, social recovery can be likened to an individual's growth through psychoanalysis. Psychology, particularly humanistic psychology, assumes that there is some redemptive potential within man, much as Morris does: the possibility of transformation is a revolutionary process. Freud and Jung, and more recently Maslow and Brown, have preached psychological sermons of the most revolutionary and romantic kind. They are, like Morris, predicting the possibility of a human ideal, the to

32

tally integrated, happy, "self-actualized" individual. Eliade highlights two key Freudian principles which are relevant here: "(1) the bliss of the 'origin' and 'beginnings' of the human being, and (2) the idea that through memory, or by a 'going back,' one can relive certain traumatic incidents of early childhood." Morris's general interest in things past, his tendency to color all his fiction with medieval trappings, and the basic plots of these early fantasies testify to his own use of the process of going back to the beginnings to recover the ends. All of this adds strength to critic Max Wickert's belief that the tools of modern psychology are absolutely necessary to a full appreciation of Morris. There is considerable need for a close reading of his fantasy writing with finely-honed contemporary psychological tools. Wickert observes that the work of Morris is full of "psychological projections," and "that an awareness of these projections, *as* projections, is important for a critical assessment of Morris's artistry; that it not only contributes to a fuller understanding, but must, in a sense, precede other kinds of analysis. The psychological projections do not form, as in much other fiction, a kind of primitive substratum to the narrative, but constitute an upper layer of significance."

We can conclude, for instance, that Morris establishes clear parallels between the psychological posture of the individual, and the collective psychology of society. There are numerous ways in which the correspondences are revealed, but the most obvious is the projection of the utopia or fantasy worlds themselves. Collective psychology is seen in mythic terms, terms which may be related to the collective unconscious of the human race as discussed by Jung. There is no division in Morris's mind between unconscious or mythical collective operations, and the collective implications of Marxism, particularly as it restates an ancient mythic pattern. Eliade points out in *Myths, Dreams and Mysteries*: "In fact, Marx's classless society, and the consequent disappearance of all historical tensions, find their most exact precedent in the myth of the Golden Age, which, according to a number of traditions, lies at the beginning and end of History. Marx has enriched this venerable myth with a truly messianic Judaeo-Christian ideology; on the one hand, by the prophetic and soteriological function he ascribes to the proletariat; and, on the other, by the final struggle between Good and Evil, which may well be compared with the apocalyptic conflict between Christ and Antichrist, ending in the decisive victory of the former. It is indeed significant that Marx turns to his own account the Judaeo-Christian hope of an *absolute* (end to) History; in that he parts company from the other historical philosophers (Croce, for instance, and Ortega y Gasset), for whom the tensions of history are implicit in the human condition, and therefore can never be completely abolished." Like many great theologians and mystics, Marx and Morris saw a blissful paradise at the beginning and end of history. For both of them, however, the vision was most definitely of "the earthly paradise," not a theoretical or heavenly one.

"The world was being brought to its second birth," Morris tells us. This is not the logical modification and evolution projected by Wells and by Bellamy, but the radically asserted claims of a millennialist. Norman Cohn has explained the political extensions of millennialism in *The Pursuit of the Millennium*, establishing Marx's position with regard to this pursuit. In presenting "The Beginning of the New Life," in *News*, Morris clearly joins the chase depicting his hopes for a new order occurring within time, but eternal in its transformation of the human condition: "The spirit of the new days, of our days, was to be delight in the life of the world; intense and overweening love of the very skin and surface of the earth on which man dwells, such as a lover has in the fair flesh of the woman he loves; this, I say, was to be the new spirit of the time. All other moods save this had been exhausted. . . . assured belief in heaven and hell as two countries in which to live, has gone, and now we do, both in word and in deed, believe in the continuous life of the world of men, and as it were, add every day of that common life to the little stock of days which our own mere individual experience wins for us: and consequently we are happy."

In our own day, our faith in "the continuous life of the world of men" is bound to have been shaken by the explosive power of atomic weaponry, by the growing threat of nuclear disaster, and by multiple environmental dangers. We may still hope for the day when there is general recognition that we have exhausted artificial and technological modes, to a time when we may turn with gladness to the overweening love of the earth. The change of consciousness required for such a social transformation is emphasized in Morris's society through its language. The new world can't be conceived in our conventional vocabulary. Many words simply have been dropped—like "school," "education," or the forgotten name of the "strange game" of power and prestige that used to be played in the Houses of Parliament where, in Morris's new society, manure is stored.

3. KILLING TIME

THE GLITTERING PLAIN

Considering attitudes toward time, history, and progress in the Nineteenth Century, the prominent critic Jerome Buckley concludes that "the great polar ideas of the Victorian period. . . were the idea of progress and the idea of decadence, the twin aspects of an all-encompassing history." Decadence was most often defined by its preoccupation with present time and its disrespect for history. Buckley explains that, "convinced that his own fleeting experience was for him the one reality in a crumbling world, the Decadent lived wholly in time. External objects lost their solidity and became, as Pater wrote, simply 'impressions, unstable, flickering, inconsistent, which burn and are extinguished with our consciousness of them.' " This total absorption in ego-existence led to the anti-heroic art-for-art's sake in the Nineties, and to the view of aesthetics as "a game by which man distracts himself." Morris's fiction of the 1880s had dealt with both past and future time, clearly establishing his respect for history. He had also presented a consistently heroic view of contemporary life (*News from Nowhere* was a message from now/here), a view antithetical to decadence, embodying instead the strengths of vigorous millenialism. *The Glittering Plain*, published in four numbers of the *English Illustrated Magazine* in 1890, is a major departure, for here, as MacKail tells us, "the imagined world was of no place or time." Not only was this short novel proof that fiction could operate effectively beyond any realistic time reference, but it also thematically paved the way for a transcendence of time which avoided the eternal childhood of Decadence.

The Story of the Glittering Plain or the Land of Living Men is one of Morris's most charming and enthralling tales. It overcomes the heaviness of the more ponderous epic or saga-type fantasies that preceded it with action that is tight, fast-paced, and symbolically intriguing. The title bears witness to the continuing presence of landscape as a symbolic motif, but the worlds in this novel are the most far-fetched Morris has yet portrayed. The author's clear rhetorical control enables us to accept the unexpected directions of the plot, and it is nearly impossible to read the book without acknowledging the extraordinary originality of both style and story line. It is simply unlike anything else in English literature before it.

Hallblithe is a strong and handsome young man who loves a young woman called the Hostage. He is from the House of the Raven—whose emblematic black bird suggests both the wings of spiritual or imaginative flight, and the drab squawking of the pesky bird—and she is from the House of the Rose— the house of beauty, of flowering, of natural fertility close to the earth. Life is good for them both; they are from Houses which traditionally marry one another, and all seems nearly perfect. Hallblithe is as happy and carefree as his "blithe" name might indicate (it's interesting to note that "blithe" derives from a Teutonic stem meaning "to shine"—so Hallblithe is a name echoing Hall-Sun). His blithe nature could also be expressive of a rather shallow and innocent young man, "without thought or regard."

The reader is introduced to the story with a strong awareness of time. The lovers are to be wed on Midsummer Night, and the story begins "one day of early spring." The strange pilgrims who question Hallblithe are concerned, they tell him, because "the hours of our lives are waning." Even though the seasonal setting provides a comfortable time-frame, there is no connection with any historical reference, or any familiar time or place. The pilgrims are looking for an eternal realm, "the land of Living Men." Its name suggests that the land itself is only important because of the "living Men," where a single human life can go on forever. When the pilgrims ask Hallblithe if *this* is the land, he replies with amusement that it is only Cleveland by the Sea (the land in its own geographical sense), and invites the travelers to stay. Convinced that it is not a place they seek, the travelers ride off again in pursuit of "the Land where the days are many." Just after their departure, Hallblithe discovers that the Hostage has been kidnapped, and hastens to rescue her.

The journey leads Hallblithe through a ritual death and rebirth, as he leaves his utopian homeland, entering a world of lies and illusions where he must confront the puzzle of time and change. His friends at home assume him dead. Like Face-of-God, Hallblithe has no choice about his quest; it is thrust upon him. But unlike the hero of *Roots*, Hallblithe has constantly in mind the object of his pursuit—the recovery of the woman he loves—and the perplexing problem of the book is the circuitous path which he must follow in order to regain her. If in symbolic terms beauty has been separated from spiritual aspiration (in *Cleave*-Land) by concern for time, or simply by the inevitable workings of time, Morris presents a circular path which reveals that the two can be reunited. Or, to put it in terms of the millennialist approach we discovered in *News*, there is a blissful paradise at the beginning and end of history. Time must be embraced to be erased.

There is a strong suggestion here that the journey constitutes a rite of passage in which Hallblithe must prove his manhood before his marriage can be consummated. Although "not untried in battle," he is first seen fashioning a spear— one of the traditional symbolic renderings of the phallus—and with the disappearance of the Hostage, he hastily completes this weapon and takes it with him, still untested, to prove its worth in the trials ahead. He embarks upon the waters, an archetypal Jungian symbol of the unconscious, and the first such watery opening in Morris's geography. The preoccupation with death which is present in each of Morris's books is best expressed by the Dantesque ferryman, Puny Fox, who leads Hallblithe to the barren Isle of Ransom, apparently a Land of the Dead. The focus of this book, which is obviously concerned with a world where the Wolfings and other "barbarians" have been defeated, is built directly on deceptive appearances, and not so much on the fundamental nature of heroism. The theme of deception and the need to distinguish between illu-

35

sion and reality begins immediately with the character of Puny Fox, whose very name belies his physical appearance. The move from Wolfing to Fox is itself an indication of a shift in heroic focus, for Puny Fox is an animal surviving on cunning and slyness, having forsaken the more direct and physical life of the primitive tribesmen.

Carole Silver, a perceptive contemporary critic, explains in her unpublished dissertation that the allegory of death-in-life, and the rite of passage through it, begins with the visit to the Isles of Ransom, which "suggests a descent to the underworld, even to the fact that the land may be approached only through an underground cave. It is a place of false values whose people honor their principle hero as 'chief liar,' and it is a place of death. That it is modeled on Iceland may at first seem surprising, but to Morris Iceland, despite its beauty, came to represent the wasteland—the bare or terrible in life or landscape." May Morris quotes an 1887 lecture in which her father refers to "the rough casket of Iceland," and this barren wintry geography was no doubt part of the formation of Icelandic myths of heroism through defeat.

Landscape in *The Glittering Plain* constitutes an extension of the bare mountaintops in some scenes of *Roots*, and may serve to remind us that Morris's redemptive visions always begin with the land and are most challenged when called upon to redeem the wasteland. Hallblithe's stay on the barren island is filled with omens and portents of death. He falls asleep shortly after his arrival, then sees an apparition of the Hostage, who speaks of taking her own life and tells him to follow her to the Land of the Living. He awakens to a "false dawn," reminded again of the illusions which surround him. The following night, after he meets the dying Sea-eagle, he witnesses a ritual battle enacted in the hall, where men dressed like his own people of the House of the Raven are slain before him.

Play-acting is a frequent habit on the island, where false illusions are presented for purposes of confusion, manipulation, and power-play. The deceits reduce human life to indistinguishable mediocrity; any single individual there can be substituted for any other. The maidens in the mime, for instance, are treated as non-entities, as "a string of women, led in by two weaponed carles." Sea-eagle confronts Hallblithe with women as mere numbers and bodies: "Tell me, my son, how many women are there in the world?" Sea-eagle simply can't understand why Hallblithe should be so much concerned about the loss of a single woman. While the difference in attitude can be partially explained as a difference between naive youth and jaded old-age, the refusal to admit special qualities of individuality is reiterated by Sea-eagle in the Acre of the Undying when, his youth restored, he dances gladly and indiscriminiately with any of the maidens. One body is as good as any other. Hallblithe can only fall back on his own instinct and intuition: "I move as one who hath no will to wend one way or other. Meseems I am drawn to go thither whereas we are going."

Hallblithe's attunement to the impulses of his inner nature is in marked contrast to the conduct of those around him. While sensing his own uniqueness, which is also a mirror for the individuality of any person (and especially of the Hostage), he actively quests for something beyond himself. Sea-eagle, on the other hand, is involved in the mere preservation of his own ego. When Hallblithe asks if Sea-eagle is looking for someone special, the old man replies, "Someone? What One? Are they not all gone? burned, and drowned, and slain and died abed? Someone, young man? Yea, forsooth some one indeed! Yea, the great warrior of the Wasters of the Shore; the Sea-eagle who bore the sword and the torch and the terror of the Ravagers over the coal-blue sea. It is myself, *myself*, that I shall find on the Land of the Glittering Plain." This absorption

36

in Self is seen as a prerequisite for happy residence in this odd land of immortality, and Sea-eagle seems well suited to the place: "But as for me I was ever an overbearing and masterful man, and meseemeth it is well that I meet as few of our kindred as may be: for they are a strifeful race."

Linked to the selfish perception of Sea-eagle and the immortalists is a rejection of the feminine principle (the Other in a male world) in favor of the merely male (Self), or a repudiation of the unconscious in favor of the rational conscious. Thus, Sea-eagle's greatest fear is his own loss of consciousness in death, while Hallblithe is perfectly willing to risk death in order to regain the Hostage. Through his pursuit of the *anima*, and the expansion of his consciousness while journeying through these lands of the dead and the living-dead, Hallblithe gains an understanding and acceptance of death, the ultimate unconsciousness. The land of Sea-eagle's dreams is clearly masculine: the realm of the Undying King, at whose command Sea-eagle has brought Hallblithe from the Isle of Ransom. It is the best reality he can imagine.

Sea-eagle agrees to assist Hallblithe, but only within the limits imposed upon him: "Not one inch beyond it may my foot go, whether it be down into the brine of the sea, or up into the clefts of the mountains which are the wall of this goodly land." For him and the other inhabitants who are trapped forever in their own egos (but are still paradoxically subject to the rule of a different King), the symbols Morris consistently uses in his geography of deliverance—water and mountain—will mean immediate death. Hallblithe, on the other hand, has his eyes already turned toward the mountains, and is not afraid of something beyond his comprehension or control. The mountains and seas formed in some distant time are images of endurance, vastness, and transcendence, psychological barriers to Sea-eagle, who is so preoccupied with living time that he is chained to it.

Nineteenth-century writers understandably devote a great deal of attention to time. With rapid developments in technology, man's sense of time was radically altered. We have seen that Morris's early fiction, as well as his own scholarly pursuits, displayed great concern for history; Buckley points out in his *Triumph of Time* that Morris's "thought and practice alike relate him to an era more strenuously devoted than any earlier one to the historical record and the historical method." Since Morris himself exercised great diligence in preserving and exploring history, it is particularly ironic that the inhabitants of the plain are compelled to forget all their history, moral instincts, and any notion of meaningful continuity in human experience. Like Tennyson's Lotos Eaters, the men of the undying land live purely for the gratification and prolongation of their individual consciousness. Rather than escaping time, these people are caught forever in time, destined to remain prisoners with no will or identity of their own, dominated and ruled by a decadent egomaniac.

The Glittering Plain, though its plot is set beyond fixed historical reality, does not abandon the value of collective history or consciousness. Most of the characters are shown to have made choices with respect to the onward march of time. The choice involves escape in the decadence of the Glittering Plain, or movement through time and ultimately beyond it. It is a dialogue with social as well as personal significance, for "Decadence was no longer simply an aspect of the common death that fallen man was heir to; it was a morbid condition of the social psyche, a disease sapping the vitality of civilization."

The Undying King is a nearly perfect figure for the Decadents who followed Morris, and who accepted part, but not the most important part, of his ideas concerning art and the beauty of life. Both the king's lavish ornament, and his own appearance ("his face shone like a star. . . when he spoke his voice was so sweet that all hearts were ravished''), describe a character who might have stepped out of a fairy tale by the arch-decadent Oscar Wilde. The king's premise is also that of the decadent—the fulfillment of every desire. The golden book is an image of art within art capturing the very image of the Hostage, writing her into a static ''love foredoomed.'' Hallblithe, unlike Sea-eagle, sees what is happening to him: ''I am accursed and beguiled; and I wander round and round in a tangle that I may not escape from. I am not far from deeming that this is a land of dreams made for my beguiling. Or has the earth become so full of lies, that there is no room amidst them for a true man to stand upon his feet and go his ways?'' Hallblithe's steadfast dedication to truth carries him through the land with his memory and purpose intact: ''I seek no dream,'' he explains, ''but rather the end of dreams.''

This statement is especially important in contrast to those who have seen Morris in his later years as an ''idle singer'' or ''dreamer of dreams.'' At the end of the book, it is Hallblithe, not the dreamer, who attains his desire. The decadent princess swooning over a picture in the golden book is an image in blatant contradiction to the social dimensions of literature which Morris constantly advocated. It is instead a mirror for the projection of self-interest and self-indulgence in limitless desire. Hallblithe's simple declaration, ''I seek no dream,'' affirms the socially-oriented mode of the fantasy genre Morris invented and designed: the central preachment is the liberation of the self from the dream.

In Hallblithe's departure from the plain via the Desert of Dread, and in his separation from Sea-eagle at the Uttermost House, the deceptions and restrictions of the plain become increasingly clear. Its duplicity is revealed in its oxymoronic name, which implies the combination of surface brilliance veneered on plain goods. Hallblithe has been disoriented with regard to time and appearance, but pushes across the waste; the weakened traveller is near death when he is rescued by the three pilgrims he encountered in the book's opening pages. His way beyond the plain must lie in a different direction.

Hallblithe therefore returns to the plain, and settles in a house at the edge of the sea, where he earns the nickname ''Wood-lover.'' His deliverance comes with his memory of ''an old song which was written round a scroll of the carving over the shut-bed, wherein he was wont to lie when he was at home in the House of the Raven.'' The song and its associated memories enable him to control the future; he plans and fashions an escape, returns to the Isle of Ransom, and recovers the Hostage. The love which joins the two reinstates reality. Even Puny Fox becomes a scholar of truth, abandoning the exercise of deception and skin-changing for which he has earned considerable reputation among his people.

The social thrust of the book is manifest in its conclusion. Hallblithe brings peace between two peoples who have lived in a perpetual state of enmity propagated by the guile of mock-battles in the Hall of the Ravagers. He returns to Cleveland-by-the-Sea, bringing with him indisputable proof of the reality through which he has passed. Puny Fox vouches for the truth of all that has happened. And when Hallblithe and the Hostage appear in the Hall, as if risen from the dead, they constitute in fact the secular trinity—father, son and holy ghost—united in love and bearing witness to the triumph of time through love, the transcendence of time through union with consciousness beyond ego.

The stream of life is affirmed in a highly symbolic ceremony at the end of the book. Erne, Puny Fox and Hallblithe mingle their blood at the earth-yoke, symbolic of the womb of the earth, and suggesting the inexhaustible source of all life (earth and blood): ''So that the blood of all three mingled together fell down on the grass of the ancient earth; and they swore friendship and brotherhood each to each." The act violates the commands of the Undying King, but it is an act of wise rebellion, sanctioned by the Ravager's own venerable sage. The flowing, the mingling, the soaking of blood into earth given freely by these "brothers"—these are images of movement and change, of identity through death. They provide a deeper understanding of death than we have yet seen in any of Morris's stories, though they all have shedding of blood. Just as death is the ultimate standard of courage, the mother of beauty in many of Morris's works, here it serves as a vehicle for true escape from time. In both of his visits to the Isles of Ransom, it is Hallblithe's nearness to death (in the company of Sea-eagle, in the presence of Puny Fox's deceased great-grandfather, and in the battle in the Hall) which makes possible his triumph. The victory can emerge in an order based on brotherhood, but never in an atmosphere of social or economic coercion.

Many critics find it curious that Morris spent his last years writing these utopian and romantic fantasies. They are, however, completely consistent with his revolutionary social vision, and represent a coming to terms with his own personality as he approached his death. *The Glittering Plain* was also the first book published by Morris's Kelmscott Press. He abandoned the cheap pamphlets of his Socialist lectures, moving instead to the lavish and expensive handmade books of a craftsman. *The Glittering Plain* marks the point where Morris firmly turns away from history and current events toward a future, not to seek an eternal life in the Land of the Undying, but to perpetuate the beauty and mystery of the unravelling patterns of life which he celebrates in the infinity of his imagination.

THE WELL AT THE WORLD'S END

Any political thinker must be concerned with means and ends, and Morris certainly was. His early stories often ended in violence or death, mediated in many of the tales by love, which prevented them from becoming pointless or purposeless. The writings of his middle years tended to focus on the strengths and failings of the love relationship as the primary human motivation. In later years, as political and social concerns came to dominate his thinking, Morris turned to the larger ends of social well-being and the selflessness of love for a wider community than a single individual. *The Well at the World's End* suggests in its title the central importance this broad concern had in his fiction. Morris's thematic concentration on the *wel*fare of the world reaches its climax in his two central works of fantasy literature, *The Well at the World's End* and *The Wood Beyond the World*, which constitute a pair in title as well as thematic concern.

Well was written in 1892-93 (though not published until 1896), and is the longest of his fantasy novels. Morris had frequently employed water as a symbol of restlessness, movement, and purification in the early fantasies; but his later novels imbue the symbol with even greater importance, suggesting a constant state of flux in the natural world, and the natural flow of the unconscious in the individual mind. *Well* takes water itself to be the object of the hero's quest, whereas, in the previous books, the flowing water had served to illustrate and complement the rooted majesty of blue-peaked mountains, often flowing down their sides, this well moves in precisely the opposite direction, penetrating the earth rather than aspiring toward the heavens. It leads us to the inner depths of Mother Earth, the source of all waters, rather than reflecting superficial geography which may shape its flow on the surface.

39

There has been confusion surrounding this piece, since the date of its conception—1892—precedes its publication date by a full four years. Hence, in most chronologies of Morris's fiction, *The Wood Beyond the World* and *Child Christopher and Goldilind the Fair* are listed erroneously as *preceding Well*. We know, however, that *Child Christopher* was not written until 1895, and was published later that same year. *Wood* was apparently begun as a story called "The King's Son and the Carle's Son." but reached a stage of disappointment after 65 pages; rather than rewrite, Morris made a new start with a different approach in another manuscript, which eventually became *Wood* in 1893. Prior to this time, in October, 1892, his secretary Sydney Cockerell was able to read 200 pages of *Well*, so the written form of the longer novel was completed relatively early, and the position of it within his ouvre must be shifted stylistically and thematically into a new perspective, as a transitional book between *The Glittering Plain* and *Wood*.

Well extends the geographical symbology so that the earth itself becomes the primary spiritual index and source of renewal, and it is important to note that this change occurs in *Well* in the explicit context of the Christian religious tradition. The story opens with the realm of King Peter, whose patriarchal kingdom serves as a foil to the quest, and a direct alternative to the matriarchal earth-kingdom which the book affirms in its conclusion. The Pre-Raphaelites never neglected Biblical subjects—Rossetti's "Annunciation" or Millais' "Christ in the House of His Parents," for instance—but they often demythologized traditional Biblical interpretations, casting the undeniably spiritual events into renewed secular perspectives. The power of the noble spiritual ideals is often heightened, in fact, by a lowering of conventional spiritual elevation, and many of the circumstances in this novel serve similar functions.

On the third page of the book we discover that King Peter's kingdom is bordered on the one side by the Wood Debateable and the other side by a Bishop and Baron of the Holy Church. King Peter's four sons are discontent within the gates of their bland paradise, and draw lots to see which three will be allowed to leave. Ralph loses, and most consequently, if he follows the demands of fate, simply stay at home with his aging father and tend to the business of the kingdom. His instincts rebel, and he leaves secretly the next morning to begin his own quest for adventure.

Ralph learns by chance of the mysterious water "beyond the Dry Tree," a fluid so potent that "it saveth from weariness and wounding and sickness; and it winneth love from all, and maybe life everlasting." Along his journey he is given the charm of a special beaded necklace, almost like a rosary, to identify his quest and bring him good fortune. The objects of the quest are clearly formulated in traditional Christian images: prayerful pilgrimage (the beads), crucifixion and sacrifice (the Dry Tree), and salvation (baptism-resurrection-the well). the post-Christian era is bound to color our reading of the emblems, and even the historic reality at the outer edge of King Peter's realm, where the Bishop holds sway; but the essential thrust of the book is in the opposite direction. Ralph heads not towards the Bishop, but towards the forest, and the tree and the well are images of the earth, not icons of heaven. Morris wishes us to see the vitality of the mysterious or mythic dimension worthy of inspiring a quest even in a post-Christian era. He doesn't want to contradict the fundamental ideals of love, goodness, decency, and forgiveness. He deplored the Christian destruction of Northern mythology, not because the Christian myths were evil and wrong, but only because they impoverished human history and imagination; by eliminating variant mythologies, Christianity made our choices fewer, our thought more narrow.

Each of Morris's later tales develops the archetypal quest motif to demonstrate the largeness of mythic variety the mind can entertain. He tried to establish good and noble examples capable of removing us from the ordinary reality we inhabit, urging us toward the realization of ideals. He was one of the earliest writers to recognize the revolutionary social ends of myth, and saw only too clearly that a destruction of mythic variety was a method of brainwashing as unhealthy as the restriction of speech or religion.

Well demonstrates the role archetypal thought plays in liberating human nature and equalizing society. The theme is embodied in the narrative through a regression to "the hermaphroditism of the child," and the final union of the two childlike and nearly bisexual characters in this tale appropriately occurs among the "Innocent Folk." In one sense, the regressive aspect is another way of exploring the millennialist Golden Age at the beginning and end of history. Increasingly hereafter in his fiction, Morris associates liberation with conjoined male and female sexuality and insists that neither role is sufficiently heroic in isolation. The ultimate object of the quest in this tale is water—an element whose feminine properties as the origin of life and symbol of unconsciousness represent completion for the masculine Ralph. The very formlessness, fluidity, and changeableness of water suggests that the sex categories may ideally share in this fluidity. When one drinks from the well, and the water becomes part of one's body, we have another form of the hermaphroditic motif.

For Morris, the hermaphroditic dimension becomes an archetypal image of the union of all things, the oneness or identity of opposites. Moreover, it is an appearance which belies reality, and by casting doubt upon our basic assumptions about sexual identity, causes us to question our stereotypes about rational, social, and political dimensions as well. Ursula frequently attires herself like a man, and is mistaken for a male by those who see her. Jung describes the hermaphrodite as the most profound "symbol of the creative union of opposites," a "uniting symbol" pointing forward to a goal not yet reached and apparently impossible. By recalling the old Platonic tale of the origin of man and woman in the original Hermaphrodite, or the Judaeo-Christian story of woman made from man in the garden, we recognize that the symbol of dichotomies arising from one flesh has been traditionally part of our mythical past, and, by the millennialist projection, could be expected to unite again in the future.

Particularly in the early sections of the book, the *anima*, or feminine instinct, is allowed to replace the patriarchal structure of the Judaeo-Christian tradition. Ralph moves past masculine feminine androgynes and pursues the Lady who has drunk of the water of the Well at the World's End; they are finally united in the "Chamber of Love in the Wilderness." Though he has been mystified by the Lady who rules as a king in the Land of the Tower (a sexual confusion in itself: "great is thy Kingship, Lady"), and has been warned against her in the worldly Burg of the Four Firths ("she is their goddess, their mawmet, their devil, the very heart and soul of their wickedness"), he joins himself to her in the cave-womb of their love bower. The cave takes him deep into the body of the earth itself, and the scene, foreshadowing the pagan equivalents of both baptism and salvation/communion, is filled with water images: "The little stream that runs yonder beneath those cliffs, is making its way towards that big river. . . O fair boy! the crossing will be to-morrow. . . "

In a shocking reversal, the Knight of the Sun appears, (note the use of punning oxymoronic/night-sun and the male sun-god), and after brutally slaying the Lady, he turns "at once upon Ralph, shaking his sword in the air (and there was blood upon the blade) and he cried out in a terrible voice: 'The witch is dead, the whore is dead! And thou, thief, who has stolen her from me, and lain by her in the wilderness, now shalt thou die, thou!'" Ralph faces both defloration and psychic castration. His response is a strong assertion of his own masculinity: "Scarce had he spoken than Ralph drew his bow to the arrow-head and loosed; there was but some twenty paces betwixt them, and the shaft, sped by that fell archer, smote the huge man through the eye into the brain, and he fell down along clattering, dead without a word more." The severe shock of the experience lets Ralph see clearly that he cannot simply follow his will (as he did when he snuck away from his father's house); and it reminds him that, as Jung observes, "the mystery of regeneration is of an awe-inspiring nature: it is a deadly embrace. There is an allusion to the terrible mother of heroes, who teaches them fear."

Ralph continues, meeting his brother Blaise, moving through the world of commerce, until finally he is captured by the Lord of Utterbol. There are many similarities between Utterbol and the land of the Undying King; Morfinn and the decadence there must be avoided. In a marvelously wrought scene with Agatha, Ralph is delivered from the entrapment of Utterbol, and comes to the realization that "I may not help everyone." He will not have completed his education as hero until he recognizes both his useful potential and the limitations imposed by his human nature. Here, unlike the Land of the Undying King success in the quest does not mean immortality, for "the water of that Well shall cause a man to thrive in all ways, and to live through many generations of men, maybe, in honour and good-liking; but it may not keep any man alive for ever; for so have the Gods given us the gift of death lest we weary of life."

The intent of long life is that the good souls who drink from the well (having of course, educated and proven themselves before reaching the end of their journey) will contribute to the general liberation of society, "that ye may better serve your fellows and deliver them from the thralldom of those that be strong and unwise and unkind."

Ralph and Ursula perservere in their quest because they seek to promote liberation and union, an event symbolized in their own marriage, and their toasts as they sip from the well reflect both their innocence (Ursula's "eye looked out of the cup the while, like a child's") and their commitment to the Mother Earth (Ralph's toast is "To the Earth, and the World of Manfolk!") As they take the road back, Ursula garbs herself again as a man, but with the consummation of their marriage, the apparent hermaphrodite has been made one flesh with the male husband. The improvement in the world during their return becomes an index of their own growth. As Jung explains in archetypal psychological terms, "As civilization develops, the bisexual primordial being turns into a symbol of the unity of personality, a symbol of the self, where the war of opposites finds peace. In this way the primordial being becomes the distant goal of man's self-development, having been from the very beginning projection of his unconscious wholeness. Wholeness consists in the union of the conscious and the unconsciousness personality."

Max Wickert suggests that Ralph may be the prototype of the artist "seeking for the grail of 'true' inspiration," and he believes that "his passage through Utterness is the last trial in the artist's ever-repeated initiation." It is worth noting that Ralph passes through Utterness twice, coming and going, and the improvement in the land on his return is not really a matter of his direct doing but almost a sympathetic response which mirrors his artistic breakthrough. Ralph contributes to human welfare in life, not merely in art; this is made manifest in a joining of "the self with the world." True, he learns much from the books he studies during his quest (once he has figured out the deceptions and lies in them and learned to read their symbols correctly), but his art is expressed through his deeds in life. The wisdom he attains for his extended lifetime consists in the recognition and application of the archetypal imaginative patterns which mediate through the experience of all generations of men, and which are, fortunately, revealed by the examples of the finest human heroes.

May Morris says of her father that "He approached life as an artist and as such felt that it was social organization, not a medley of individual efforts— that in random struggle no great work could ever be achieved: sincere art could only come from the free man, bound by his debt to Life itself!" Ralph reflects this orientation after he is indeed bound to Life at the well. The great symbol of the Dry Tree, itself androgynous, sums up the great advance in the years which separate us from the *House of the Wolfings*. This tale, Morris hopes, may begin to show how to make the waste land bloom again, and how to make a house our home:

> *"The Dry Tree shall be seen*
> *On the green earth, and green*
> *The Well-spring shall arise*
> *For the hope of the wise.*
> *They are one which were twain,*
> *The Tree bloometh again,*
> *And the Well-spring hath come*
> *From the waste to the home."*

4. BEYOND THE WORLD

How does one take the reader beyond the world? That question plagued Morris from the first, in his poetry, fiction, decorative work, and political activities. He consistently sensed the truth embodied in the Christian paradox that one must lose one's life to save it, and his Romantic inclinations coupled with his strongly humanistic convictions led him to the intuitive belief that one must lose the world to save it. Dream, of course, is one way the mind releases its hard grasp on known reality, and the cleansing and renewing effect of sleep (and dreaming even during day-dream reveries) were long recognized as good methods for renewal and creative discovery. Morris's earliest stories seem to have tried to shake or shock the reader into a departure from known reality, in an effort to disrupt the normal, expected patterns of thought, and enable the mind to reform itself. In the later and longer fictions, Morris employed the dream-tale and historical displacement to ease his readers into a world beyond the world which might cleanse and renew their doors of perception and conception. *The Well at the World's End* and *The Wood Beyond the World* were reversed in order of publication for a number of reasons, including the great length of *Well*; more important may have been the critical reception accorded *The Glittering Plain*. From the time his first fantasies appeared, Morris was accused of turning his back on the political and social reforms he had so intensely fought for in earlier years. Having seen his readers miss the point in *The Glittering Plain*, even though he had already taken things a step further in *Well*, it must have seemed to Morris that he needed to retreat. He could perhaps make more direct connections and parallels between familiar worldly concerns and the fictional events, leading his readers to see more clearly the millennial possibility he so desired.

THE WOOD BEYOND THE WORLD

The Wood Beyond the World represents a transitional style for Morris in a conceptual sense: he is still experimenting with how far to push the "transition" to the fantasy realm. The opening of the novel stresses an ordinary and mundane reality—Golden Walter is a wealthy eligible son snatched up by a woman who is probably a social climber. A relative innocent, he feels strong sexual attraction for her; she gratifies his desire, but at the same time services a select company of attractive young men in the town. He finds himself unable to continue in this kind of situation. The opening scene with his father is quite credible in its realism; the father asks first if she is pregnant.

When Walter makes up his mind to leave, directing his energy toward the boundless sea (limitless possibility for the future), he begins to see, or to hallucinate, the three weird figures who eventually become his primary reality. Whether they are real or imaginary is interestingly in doubt. A verification of their existence occurs when they are witnessed and described by the accountant who comes to deliver the news that Walter's father is dead. But even then, with the group suddenly disappearing, there is still the possibility of simultaneous hallucination.

Throughout this opening section there is a curious tension between language and circumstance. The direct, rhythmic, and "artificial" (in the best sense) prose counterpoints a sordid and mundane state of affairs. From the very beginning, the elevated language used to describe a sordid and ordinary marriage gives us a sense of the book's direction: by altering our perspective, we can enhance our ability to alter our destiny and bring it more in line with our ideals. The realistic novel moves in precisely the opposite direction. The roughness of contemporary life—exemplified by particularly explicit sexuality—is rendered in profane and mundane literalness. Transcripts of the Nixon tapes, complete with expletives, show how low life and low language cling to one another. Morris uses the vocabulary, syntax, and rhythm of his writing to avoid the everyday, predictable, or expected, encouraging an elevation in language which may in turn elevate our thoughts and aspirations.

Wood is the only one of his fantasies prompted by an unfaithful woman. Golden Walter undertakes his journey to escape the negative feminine instinct of pure desire without the virtues of faithfulness, love, or idealism. Earlier, Morris's hero was prompted to the quest by defense of country, or the protection of love; but here he is driven from a land of commercialism by the threat of a future generation, promulgated by unregulated desire without loyalty, appetite without identity. Morris is quite frank about the situation, without sacrificing his style. Walter's father asks him whether or not his wife is pregnant: the lad responds, "I wot not; nor of whom the child may be." Walter finds the situation intolerable and knows there must be something better. He decides to clarify his purpose and identity, and while he is not clear regarding his ultimate objective, he does seek to establish his masculine identity: "Yet if we do meet, father, then shalt thou see a new man in me."

They never meet again. This is the first time a hero does not return to his tribe or people at the end of a Morris novel. And here is another reason why one should recognize that this book, published before *Well*, thematically and stylistically comes after it. Increasingly, Morris looks to his heroes to forge and form their own identities, and to establish a new order within a larger human family where the insights of the hero and heroine can be promulgated. Once Walter has decided to sail away—the journey by water suggests an entrance into the unconscious—he moves ever closer to a place he has never seen, and ends his life as ruler of a people who are strange to him. The omens or phantoms which lead him forward include a dark, hideous dwarf, a grey-eyed young maiden with an iron ring on her ankle, and a glorious lady, tall and beautiful.

With his ship blown off course by winds beyond his control, Walter will be drawn into an adventure with these mysterious figures. Coming to an unknown land, he meets a primitive man clad in skins and learns about the tribe of "Bears" who serve a mysterious and powerful lady as their god. After traversing a rocky mountainous wall, he sees before him a terrible waste land, and later discovers a "strange and sweet land" where he meets the maiden dressed all in green, a woman who begs to be delivered from a plight common to many of Morris's characters, "from this death in life." Realizing that they are both caught in nets of deception, they vow to help one another even through deceitful means, and to forgive these deceptions later (ends justifying means, in Marxian terms?). Finally, Walter discovers a house "with gold and fair hues," with a roof of "tiles. . . of yellow metal, which he deemed to be of very gold," and "a fountain of gold, whence the water ran two ways in gold-lined runnels." Here lives the wondrous lady clad in gold and jewels.

The rich house and its trappings give clear indication of the great isolation from nature this environment represents. It connotes high artificiality, exemplified in the decadence of the Lady who is "walking with the King's Son, and he clad in thin and wanton raiment, but she in nought else save what God had given her of long, crispy yellow hair." The difference between the Lady and the Maid is accentuated by the Lady's manipulation of clothing (and the lack thereof) to alter her appearance as it suits her; Walter finds himself "astonished at the change which had come over her," while the Maid "was clad even as she was before, and changed in no wise." Sexual faithfulness and physical constancy in dress and appearance are linked symbolically in the book, just as the sexual promiscuity in the opening pages seems to be associated with the urban and commercial life of which Golden Walter is the offspring. Images of gold in the tale suggest deceptive potential; as in *The Glittering Plain*, all that glitters is not gold.

The dwarf, the maid, and the Lady constitute a deceptive trinity. They seem to operate on a transcendent plane, where the Lady is worshiped as a God. Though she seems to dress "as the hunting-goddess" at one point, and is clearly associated with Diana and concupiscence, the Lady is obviously helpless in confrontation with the lion, an image of the raw force of nature. Her smooth and polished speeches are reduced to "a kind of gibbering cry without words." By slaying the King of beasts to rescue the Lady, Walter symbolically slays her incestuous current lover, who is both king and son. Straightening out this situation is a way of compensating or balancing the unfaithfulness of his own wife. If the feminine principle represents sexual desire alone, it is bound to lead to decadent rule, "dwarfing" the only man who can remain loyal under the circumstances.

Walter moves through numerous deaths and murders in the course of the story. His leaving home seems to lead indirectly to his own father's death—there are some slight parallels to *Hamlet*. He later slays the lion, and then supports the Maid as she liberates herself from her Lady "mother's" evil slavery. Finally, he kills the dwarf in a particularly ugly scene, burying the "Evil Thing" with its head by its buttocks, to make certain it is irrevocably dead. The dwarf (recall the dwarf-wrought hauberk which tempted Thiodolf) seems consistently

45

a negative image in Morris, an image of man diminished, degraded, perverted, subjected, and tyrannized.

But Walter's "murder" of his father is accidental, and his first direct killing turns out to be a phantom. It is only when he is teamed with the Maid that he gains stature as an effective heroic force, suggesting that neither the male nor female instincts, neither the conscious nor unconscious mind, is effective in isolation. The murders in the book are inevitable as part of a revolution to escape oppression. The daughter (the Maid) has been enslaved by the mother— just as Walter had been caught in the "Golden" commercialism of his father with a glamorous but promiscuous wife. The heroism of the book is shared by the couple, and the main thrust is toward liberation of the repressed feminine principle, important since the Maid compensates ultimately for the promiscuous habits of Walter's wife.

By the end of the book Walter drops the "Golden" from his name, and is moving, in Jung's terms, "from a sexual system into an intellectual or spiritual system." The Maid magically demonstrates, in fact, the spiritual redirection of sexual energy when her very touch is able to bring wilted flowers to life. Unlike her masters, the dwarf and the Lady who represent deformed moral and physical humanity, the Maid (with Walter) emphasizes a balanced spiritual and physical union: "Thus we say to each other; and to God and his Hallows we say: 'We two have conspired to slay the woman who tormented one of us, and would have slain the other; and if we have done amiss therein, then shall we two together pay the penalty; for in this have we done as one body and one soul.' "

Before they can safely conclude their escape, Walter and the Maid must journey through the hill-country of the Bear-folk, a primitive people close to the earth who had worshipped the mistress as a God. But the Maid demonstrates a moral victory so complete that she even has command of time, together with a close attunement with Nature. This is a complete reversal of the image in Shakespeare's *Hamlet*, where, physical values have overtaken spiritual ones. The Bear-folk use stone-age weapons, but their brute force is powerful enough to carry out their threat to drown the Maid should she be judged a "light liar." In a striking parallel with Ophelia, the Maid dresses herself with greenery and flowers, seeming truly to be the "Mother of Summer," complete with the power to awaken the dying flowers: "The eglantine roses opened, and all was as fresh and bright as if it were still growing on its own roots." The Maid's proclamation to the Bear-folk is one of resurrection and renewal: "Now, then, is the day of your gladness come; for the old body is dead, and I am the new body of your God, come amongst you for your welfare." Morris presents her flowery attire in vivid pictorial detail which calls to mind the minute flowers which surround Ophelia as she is swept along the river in Millais's painting. But Morris's portrait of Ophelia is victorious. There is a suggestion in *Hamlet* that if the brooding self-conscious hero could only overcome his incestuous preoccupation with his mother and improve his own conduct toward Ophelia, the outcome of Shakespeare's play might have come closer to the world "set right" toward which Morris's fantasy flows. Having moved beyond the world to find "one body and one soul" the Maid and Walter return to the world at the end of the book with a clarity and vision capable of establishing a new city. Equality is the basis for the world set right, and Morris concludes the tale with the observation that under this revolutionary new order, "folk had clean forgotten their ancient custom of king-making."

CHILD CHRISTOPHER AND GOLDILIND THE FAIR

Hamlet is a renaissance myth *par excellence*. While the tragedy is magnificent in its depiction of the human struggle between passion and intellect, public good and personal emotion, and the extremes of sexual passion and family loyalty which haunt the dreams of all our lives, it is also a story which documents the peculiarly modern character of all these troubles. The crippling isolation and introspection of the central character would not have marked the difficult life decisions faced in earlier tribal societies. At least not according to Morris, and this point he makes by returning to one of Shakespeare's sources for *Child Christopher and Goldilind the Fair*.

Though Morris may not have seen Shakespeare's hero in the thirteenth-century English metrical romance *Havelock the Dane*, he responded to its dramatic and thematic content with an imaginative extension as compelling in its own way as Shakespeare's introspective version. Composed in a Northeast Midland dialect of Middle English, *Havelok* and its surviving partner in manuscript, *King Horn*, are "the oldest surviving examples of the romance genre in English." Both stories have counterparts in earlier oral and written traditions, and versions of the two exist in 12th century Old French literature. *Havelok*, published in a scholarly edition by the Early English Text Society in 1868, appealed to Morris not only for its historical importance and Old French connections, but also because it is one of the earliest extant pieces of English literature to use the language of common people and to reach out to a non-courtly audience. The romance still retains echoes of the courtly mode (as does Morris's version), but this is understandable in any transformation of a literary mode from one class to another. Morris, who opposed the social and economic exploitation of the courtly tradition, recognized in this story of a legendary king of England and Denmark a fable with mythic and human importance.

The original tale tells of an English princess named Goldborough who is left an orphan at the age of two. While she is growing up, her kingdom is ruled by a regent appointed by her father. The regent is instructed to marry her to the best, fairest, and strongest man living, and to assure her rule as Queen when she is old enough. Instead, he shuts her up in Dover Castle. Similarly, Havelok is orphaned when his father, the King of Denmark, dies. The councilor entrusted to rule until Havelok comes of age attempts to have the young prince drowned, but a luminous mark on the boy's shoulder and a bright light issuing from his mouth convince an honest fisherman that the child must be a true king; he is spirited away to England for safekeeping, where he is raised as a simple fisherman. Finally gaining local fame in a sports contest (stonethrowing), he attracts the attention of Goldborough's regent, who decides to marry her to this poor boy. When the two are wed, and both deceitful regents feel their positions to be entirely safe, Havlok and Goldborough realize through dreams and glowing signs that they must claim their thrones. Havelok invades Denmark, regains his kingdom, and then conquers England, rewarding all those who have cared for him. He and Goldborough live a hundred years and have many children.

Morris began his career as a poet by looking, as did many of the Pre-Raphaelites, at the Arthurian tales as the primary British myth system. That myth, which Morris explored extensively in his writing, depicts an ideal kingdom overthrown through the weakness of human passions. Morris had already written nearly the opposite story in *Wolfings*, where Thiodolf resists temptation to preserve a communal society. The Arthurian myths (like *Hamlet*) lead us toward psychological introspection (which Morris perfectly reveals in "The

47

Defense of Guinevere"), while both Havelok and Thiodolf lead us toward a redeemed society, toward good government and united peoples. In adapting the tale, Morris preferred a happy ending to the tragic result of Shakespeare's play, or the rotten core of Camelot which destroyed the dream.

Morris advised his daughter that the proper way to retell an old romance was to "Read it through, then shut the book and write it out again as a new story for yourself." This provides a way of casting the narrative in your own words, while preserving the spirit of the source; it also imitates the basic method of storytelling in the oral tradition which shaped the form of these earliest romances. Morris approved the rootedness which could result from building firmly on tradition. The mixture of Old French, English, and Scandinavian influences in this tale fit him like a glove. Here was a story which ideally suited a socialist perspective beyond nationalism (Arthurian legend was strongly nationalistic). Morris had already followed his literary roots to the European continent to produce translations of three Old French romances, which he published at the Kelmscott Press starting in 1893, and his saga translations had expressed his Northern roots even earlier.

French romance techniques abound in *Child Christopher*, adding yet another important source to the emerging fantasy form which Morris was shaping. As Joseph Jacobs observed in the introduction to the 1896 edition of Morris's French translations, the historic origins were far-ranging: "The first two crusades brought the flower of European chivalry to Constantinople and restored that spiritual union between Eastern and Western Christendom that had been interrupted by the great schism of the Greek and Roman Churches. The crusaders came mostly from the Lands of Romance. Permanent bonds of culture began to be formed between the extreme East and the extreme West of Europe by intermarriage, by commerce, by the admission of the nobles of Byzantium within the orders of chivalry. These ties went on increasing throughout the twelfth century till they culminated at its close with the foundation of the Latin kingdom of Constantinople. In European literature these historic events are represented by the class of romances. . . which all trace back to versions in verse of the twelfth century." Jacobs goes on to point out that "their interlaced history reads more like a page of the *Arabian Nights* than of Gibbon," and he suggests there may be even more ancient versions of the stories going back to Arabic or Ethiopic sources.

If a man may be known by the company he keeps, the fact that Morris chose to keep these traditions alive tells us a great deal about his termperament, artistry, and vision. Critics have made a good beginning with the Old Norse sources (*William Morris and Old Norse Literature* by J. N. Swannell, William Morris Society, 1961) but the Old French tales must be seen as nearly equal in impact. And the tracing of Byzantine, Persian, Arabic, and other Eastern roots in many of his arts—carpet and fabric design, manuscript and book illumination, poetry and fiction—has scarcely begun. This is partly due to the absence today of the very "bonds of culture" which are celebrated in the tales, but one cannot study Morris without being led again and again to explore Eastern patterns of culture. "Out of Byzantium by Old France," as Jacobs tells us, "is a good strain by which to produce thoroughbred romance," and it is an enormous credit to Morris that he passes these origins, ancient and profound, to the great practitioners of the fantasy form in the 20th century, especially C. S. Lewis and J. R. R. Tolkien, both of whom acknowledged their indebtedness.

Jacobs further notes that the characteristics of the Old French Romance which Morris brought into his own fantasy, especially in *Child Christopher*, are "the very air of romance. . . . There is none of your modern priggish care for

48

the state of your soul. . . .Adventures are to the adventurous, and the world is full of them. Every place but that in which one is born is equally strange and wondrous. Once beyond the bounds of the city walls and none knows what may happen. We have stepped forth into the Land of Faerie, but at least we are in the open air.'' This is the openness Morris had already developed in his own fiction, and he conveys it again in this retelling of *Child Christopher*: ''Wonder and reverence, are not these the parents of Romance? Intelligent curiosity and intellectual doubt—those are what the Renaissance brought.''

The spirit of the original 1895 Kelmscott Press edition of *Child Christopher* is reminiscent of the historical antecedents which inform it. The title page, with lettering, floral illumination, and decoration by Morris himself, beautifully combines both Eastern and Western influences. Here, as throughout his life (and especially in the fantasy novels which he designed and printed), there is a vision of unity wedding the visual and literary arts; it is a synthesis widely practiced in the East, where calligraphic decorations are used in architecture and in the highest art forms, and where stories often hinge upon slight nuances in spelling or calligraphy, or upon a pun which reveals the slippery and deceptive nature of language. On his Kelmscott Press title page (reproduced in the Newcastle paperback edition) Morris rearranges the order of words to emphasize visual and thematic balances:

> *''Of Child*
> *Christo-*
> *pher and*
> *Fair Gold*
> *ilind''*

If we read the words in the way Morris has arranged them, we are strongly drawn to the *''Christo''* in *''Christopher,''* and led to implications of spiritual salvation.

As a linguist and translator, Morris enjoyed the roots of language as an affirmation of the continuity and progression of human culture, a delight he shared with Tolkien. He chose to stress these roots in both his prose style and word choice, and his unusual style, which seems so odd and uniform at first, actually varies considerably from book to book, uniquely reflecting the atmosphere, tradition, and theme of each tale. The name ''Christopher'' derives from Greek, through Latin and Old French, and means ''bearer of Christ.'' Originally the word was applied by the Christians to themselves, meaning that they bore Christ in their hearts. Later, St. Christopher came to prominence, an early Christian martyr whose name was attached to the legend of a holy man who carried the child Christ across a river—an action which is interesting to bear in mind in light of the river which so often cleaves or divides or isolates humanity in Morris's fiction. Particularly in his final book, *The Sundering Flood*, Morris is diligently concerned to find a way of overcoming the sundering of human nature, and St. Christopher bridges the dividing barrier of the water. Always the patron of travellers, St. Christopher was one of the commonest subjects for mural paintings inside English churches, and a favorite saint of the man-on-the-street. Morris, who departed from conventional religion at college, was attracted by the human emphasis in the story. A Morris and Co. stained-glass window depicting Saint Christopher was designed in 1868 by Burne-Jones and executed in rich colors by Morris. It is one of the most artistically successful small windows ever executed by the firm, and emphasizes the human commitment of Christopher, a good man who stooped to carry the burden of a fellow traveller across a difficult impasse. In the context of Morris's tale the name and image seem clearly to connote human spirituality in relation to one's fellow man.

The central lines of Morris's calligraphic title page arrangement provide visual connection and support, with "pher" arranged symmetrically above the following line and hinting at a rhyme between *"pher"* and *"fair."* *"Gold,"* so often associated with money and material wealth in Morris's fiction, is joined in the heroine's name with fairness, not greed or exploitation. The spiritual emphasis of Christopher is linked to the material fairness of Goldilind. The final syllables, *"ilind,"* suggest *"island,"* a reference to England and an old name for Iceland, so that the Old French linguistic roots in *"Christopher"* are wedded to old Icelandic roots in *"Goldilind"*; *"I lend,"* which connotes the supportive dimension Goldilind gives to the union in the book; and *"lind,"* a Middle-English word for tree (used, for instance, by Chaucer in his "Clerk's Tale," *"Be ay of chere as light as leef on linde"*). This final sense of *"tree"* leads us to the unifying natural growth motifs present on the title page through the illumination, and the decorative and literary images of natural growth throughout the narrative. The language of the title page is caressed and embraced and even supported, but not hidden, in natural illumination which ranges from delicate leaf and floral patterns at the center to more vigorous, flowing acanthus spirals at the outer border. It shows kinship with the finest Persian illuminated manuscripts as well as medieval Celtic and Continental illumination. The page forms a whole, graceful and lively, a wedding of Eastern and Western traditions of spiritual and material planes, of the unconscious flowing growth of nature with the rational consciousness expressed through language.

We might expect, just from this close examination of the title page, that the narrative would portray an ideal world of natural, human, spiritual balance, and the opening scenes confirm this notion. The book begins in Oakenrealm, another wood beyond the world. It is a country "which was so much a woodland, that a minstrel thereof said it that a squirrel might go from end to end, and all about, from tree to tree, and never touch the earth." In the opening action we find ourselves in a dense wood, but one unlike the dark, confused forest of Dante at the beginning of the *Inferno*. Instead, this wood provides a haven for tiny creatures, and focuses our attention on the protective upper branches, like the dome of heaven itself, where our thoughts, with the squirrel, need not touch the earth. While our thoughts are elevated, they are still tied to the earth; supported by the sturdy tree-trunks, unifying branches span the land "from end to end." The imagination is not directed to a distant heaven, but to a higher plane in touch with nature.

This forest kingdom of Oakenrealm is home to Child Christopher, and the trees are symbolic, as they have been from Yggdrasill (the great ash tree in Norse mythology whose roots and branches hold together the universe) to the Christian Tree of Life, suggesting a spiritual as well as a natural domain. In marked contrast to the Dry Tree in his previous *Wood*, Morris here presents a lush and fertile tree, a vision of nature (and ultimately of natural fate or destiny) supporting, sheltering, uplifting the life within it. Goldilind, despite the *"lind"* of her name, is from Meadham, a level plain close to flat ground, and therefore suggestive of the material realm, the glittering plain. When she encounters Christopher later in the story, it is Goldilind who will be most concerned with appearances and rich position. Though each of these central characters is tagged with the name of a dwelling place, they are both dispossessed of their rightful inheritance and assume functions opposite to their tag images. In their actions Christopher and Goldilind approximate the archetypal *animus* and *anima* of Jungian psychology, the active rational and creative unconscious forces of the psyche. Only when they are united is their success assured, and in their union the spiritual and material, unconscious and conscious, are wed. As political and social commentary, the story suggests that the sons and daughters of modern society are deprived of their rightful inheritance by corrupt establishments. More specifically for the English heritage in myth, politics, and language, it makes us aware that we have been all but dispossessed of our French and Northern roots. It illustrates the importance of reuniting the fragmented and dislocated children (and traditions), and affirms the ultimate inevitability of their union.

Fate makes a strong appearance in *Child Christopher*, but it is not a fate to fear, as it is in so many of the earlier stories. In his short stories, Morris's characters seemed to move powerless within the driven limits of their destinies; in *Wolfings*, and the early fantasies, Morris applauds the individual hero precisely because he assumes the lost cause and gives his life in its behalf. Here we have the fate and hero drawn into one accord. It is the uplifting prospect which Morris praised in the finest imaginative writing: the "would-be" is brought to reality through heroic work.

THE WATER OF THE WONDROUS ISLES

It is part of the romance tradition that a hero and heroine should wed at the end of the story. The whole point about romance is that it moves from isolation to union, from conflict to community. It is interesting to reflect upon Morris's fiction from the standpoint of endings alone. In the short stories we often read of violent destruction and abrupt fatalistic or arbitrary death. The youthful Morris reflects in his writing the perceptions of his own time, a period filled with arbitrary destruction, ancient architecture demolished, traditions overturned, and individuals dehumanized by technology. He also witnessed the obliteration or irrevocable alteration of whole cultures by the British version of the Roman Empire. There is a noticeable change of attitude in the longer fiction of Morris's last years, where characters conclude their lives in union with a tribe, a folk, or a new society. A final shift occurs in the last few novels, where the protagonists are separated or divided at the start, and united male to female (sometimes in a single body, and conveyed through androgynous images) at the conclusion. Despite the abstract quality which all of the novels maintain, they do become increasingly personal and psychological. Morris seems to have united in the final tales an interlinked perception of theories individually explained by Freud and Jung in psychology and by Marx in politics. He is one of the earliest writers to assert metaphorically that an integrated psyche and a utopian society are inextricably bound. We may call the two sides *animus* and *anima*, thesis and antithesis, or see them mirrored in the courageous stoicism and the Gothic tongue of the saga-man and the courtly grace of the Old French romance. Again and again, the reader is asked to ponder the two made one; repeatedly, the narrator shows us the challenge, the heroism, and the joy of union as the tale tells us once again that there is indeed a happy ending.

The Water of the Wondrous Isles is Morris's longest and most complex investigation of the feminine consciousness or *anima*. It is plainly a novel about women's liberation. While the male heroes in most of his other tales are heavily armed and armored (even the woman of *Well* wears man's armor throughout much of the story), Birdalone is first pictured as a nearly naked infant, and remains unclothed in some of the most critical scenes of the book. In this novel the defenses are down. The central figure of this fantasy is a woman, and Morris sensitively follows her from vulnerable, bird-like aloneness, to her dis-

51

covery of a strong internal self. It is not armor which provides a hero's health, strength, and defense, Morris seems to say—nor armor which protects or improves a society—but a realization of the fullness of human experience, and an insistence in joining fragmented and limited lives into triumphant wholes. Contemporary psychology borrows the term "armoring" as a way of designating the protective defense mechanisms of the neurotic personality. In this novel Morris shows us his most psychologically healthy male hero (Hugh) overcoming the most thoroughly evil female demon (the Witch-wife's sister) while completely nude.

The story opens in "a walled cheaping-town hight Utterhay," a setting which embodies all the evil aspects associated with "utter" states in Morris's fiction. Geographically, it reverses the woodland setting of *Child Christopher* and the *Wood,* for it begins in the city which is bounded by a vast wood the inhabitants believe filled with demons, a wood called *"Evilshaw,"* that might be "great, or maybe measureless." As an example of the town's corruptness, we are shown "a babe of some two winters, which was crawling about on its hands and knees, with scarce a rag upon its little body." The child's mother has "a face which had once been full fair, but was now grown bony and haggard, though she were scarce past five and twenty years." The social system is indicted by the woman's complaint: "What neighbors have I since my man died; and I dying of hunger, and in this town of thrift and abundance." Morris is characteristically ahead of his time in recognizing the repression of women in society as a mirror of our most dominant individual neurosis: the severe repression of the unconscious.

Particularly in his last two fantasy novels, Morris achieves a total integration of archetypal fantasy metaphor with social commentary. The symbolic actions of his characters reveal a provocative psychological glimpse into an age sorely lacking in visionary imagination, either in political or literary terms. The realistic social misery at the beginning of *The Water of the Wondrous Isles* might easily be found in industrial London, and the islands of the title are bound to suggest the island nation of Britain itself. But the opening scene is immediately countered with an unwomanly stranger, "tall and strong of aspect. . . black-haired, hook-nosed and hawk-eyed, not so fair to look on as masterful and proud," who steals a child and carries her off to Evilshaw. For the little girl, Birdalone, it is both the beginning of capitivity and the beginning of liberation.

In *The House of the Wolfings*, Morris showed us the men in combat, while the women, conspicuously present, played no real part in the central conflict between the Roman and tribal wolves. *Water* employs a similar contrast to delineate two aspects of contact with the unconscious in its bright and evil sides. The image of the bird takes on strikingly different aspects in the hawk-eyed Witch-wife and the innocent Birdalone: one is a bird of prey and the other a caged captive. Even the deceptive art of skin-changing (perhaps an allusion to cosmetics) does little to render the Witch-wife more attractive; and when she assumes her customary appearance, she is "flat-breasted. . . and narrow-hipped." Her hook-nosed face reveals a sterile masculinity imposed upon what might have been a more fruitful feminine frame; her sterility is doubly evident in her theft of the child she is unable to bear herself. Birds, like angels, are traditionally symbolic of spiritualization and the soul, and also of creative thought, flights of imagination, and aspiration. At the beginning of the tale the infant Birdalone is downcast: her father is dead, her mother impoverished, and she is separated by deception from her real family roots, from her identity as a woman, by the tyranny of the flat-breasted witch. Birdalone is trapped, forced to live at the end of a great lake (the unconscious); from both the individual and the social view, the situation is grim.

Morris's novels usually portray the search of an active, dynamic male hero (rational consciousness) for the discovery or recovery of a more passive, imaginative feminine heroine (*anima*, or the unconscious); this quest usually establishes a union which transcends isolated or alienated experience. In *Water*, however, the feminine principles are helplessly passive within the rich and materialistic society, and Birdalone is captured by a symbol of evil femininity turned upon itself—the Witch-wife is raising the child so that she will "grow into the doing of my will." The individual will, with the motivation and direction it provides, plays a part in many of the earlier fantasy tales; here the evil subconscious (Witch-wife) tries from the outset to subvert Birdalone's intuitive spiritual will toward goodness.

Birdalone's journey toward freedom begins in a narcissistic (or even homosexual) encounter with Habundia in the midst of the woods, in the depths of the natural world where the Witch-wife dares not venture. Habundia is a more or less standard figure from allegorical romance, suggestive of Dame Habond in *Le Roman de la Rose*; she also possesses many characteristics of the Germanic goddess Habundia, as depicted in a book Morris admired from his Oxford days, Jacob Grimm's *Teutonic Mythology*. In *Water* Habundia appears frequently in the exact image of Birdalone, enacting the role of an ancient and wise *anima* figure. Birdalone is sitting naked in the woods, sewing the green fabric of her first womanly gown when "she saw standing before her the shape of a young woman naked as herself, save that she had an oak-wreath round about her loins." Since Birdalone has been forbidden a mirror, and is not allowed even a brief glimpse of her own image, the visually descriptive and sensuous scene in which Habundia tells her, "now am I to be thy mirror," is a first recognition of her own identity. This first real glimpse of herself may be, in some ways, the truest perception she will ever enjoy: "My friend, when thou hast a mirror, some of all this shalt thou see, but not all; and when thou hast a lover some deal wilt thou hear, but not all. But now thy she-friend may tell it thee all, if she have eyes to see it, as have I; whereas no man could say so much of thee before the mere love should overtake him, and turn his speech into the folly of love and the madness of desire."

Shortly after this first self-awakening, Birdalone goes far out swimming in the great waters; "Then she communed with herself, and found that she was thinking: If I might only swim all the water and be free." The total immersion in the vastness of unconscious experience, especially as she gains self-consciousness for the first time, is awesome and naive. The idea of swimming to freedom is an impossible one, but as she returns to land, her discovery of a boat at the mouth of a creek offers a more realistic vehicle for her deliverance. The passage describing the discovery of the Sending Boat reflects both her innocence and her innate good sense: "Close on the mouth of the creek, on Birdalone's side thereof, lay a thing floating on the dull water, which she knew not how to call a boat, for such had she never seen, nor heard of, but which indeed was a boat, oarless and sailless. She looked on it all about, and wondered; yet she saw at once that it was for wending the water, and she thought, might she but have a long pole, she might push it about the shallow parts of the lake, and belike take much fish." Her isolation cries out for an instrument beyond herself—in this case the long pole is only one of many images of phallic male identity which will become part of Birdalone's liberation.

This heroine is remarkable among Morris's characters in that she is raised entirely by women and is calculatedly brainwashed by the Witch-wife. Her success as a heroine lies in discovering herself and journeying beyond the world she knows toward a union with something greater, a truly amazing emergence of consciousness from near absolute repression. Morris's tale, when considered from the aspect of social commentary, depicts the spirit of the age in its collective repression of the unconscious and its symbolic downtrodden woman (Rossetti's "Jenny" is another Pre-Raphaelite example), one similar to those who might be found in London or any other metropolitan center. Recalling that Liberty is a woman in the French tradition, one senses even more strongly the difficulty of liberating repressed human freedom from the old witch: "The Witch-wife sprang up and turned on her with a snarl as of an evil dog, and her face changed horribly: her teeth showed grinning, her eyes goggled in her head, her brow was all too-furrowed, and her hands clenched like iron springs. Birdalone shuddered back from her and cringed in mere terror, but had no might to cry out. The witch hauled her up by the hair, and dragged her head back so that her throat lay bare before her all along. Then drew the witch a sharp knife from her girdle, and raised her hand over her, growling and snarling like a wolf."

The phallic knife associates the scene with bestial, violent, demonic, sadistic sexuality. Birdalone, made to drink a secret potion, is lectured severely and finds herself traumatically transformed into a milk-white hind. Fifteen days later she awakens in her bed with the vague feeling that it might have been a dream, but the witch's horrible lesson is still clear to her: "If thou pry into my matters, and lay bare that which I will have hidden, then . . . I must be avenged on thee even to slaying."

The incident in another context might seem merely a parent-child (mother-daughter) conflict carried to neurotic extremes. There is also the suggestion of a Biblical parallel, with Birdalone, like Eve, tempted to test forbidden knowledge. Yet, like all the gods who inevitably seem to be overthrown by their offspring, the Witch-wife inwardly "began to fear Birdalone." At the center of Birdalone's experience is the tree, her own tree of knowledge in the Oak of Tryst, once again a prominent center in Morris's fiction. Birdalone continues to meet Habundia at the Oak, and to learn from her. She also receives a magic ring, which can cause her to become invisible, and with its aid follows the witch to her boat, learning the secret of its operation. The stern and bow must be covered with blood, the flowing of which will signify an end to her innocent childhood. By the end of the book many streams of blood have mingled on the boat, and with it the streams of the narrative; the human river of life drives the heroine to cross the waters of the unconscious, to navigate and hence surmount them, to join the adult human race. Birdalone boards the boat naked, plucks her fair skin with a thorn to make the boat carry her away, and thereby wounds herself into consciousness. Her escape scene is delightful and painful simultaneously, and the conclusion cries out to be filmed: "There the witch stood tossing her arms and screaming, wordless; but no more of her saw Birdalone, for the boat came round about the ness of Green Eyeot, and there lay the Great Water under the summer heavens all wide and landless before her."

The boat carries Birdalone to an island where she meets three good sisters; unfortunately this new land is ruled by the Witch-wife's sister, "crueller than the cruellest." We discover, along with Birdalone, that the imprisonment of women is not limited to one woman alone. In conversation with the maidens, Birdalone finds the one flaw of the tyrannical sorceress: the red witch has a short memory. Since the witch is, like the Undying King or the Lord of Utterbol, a figure to be identified with decadence, her short memory serves to disconnect her from the past, showing us the vulnerablity of isolation in present-time self-indulgence. Birdalone's knowledge enables her to continue her journey through the Isles of the Young and the Old, where there is no maturity, only death and helpless infancy. And she moves through the Isles of Queens and the Isle of Kings as through a wax museum, witnessing the death-in-life of petrified sexuality.

These islands, with a capstone Isle of Nothing, bear witness to the hopelessness of separation, for on the final Isle Birdalone recognizes "that in that dull land, every piece thereof was like every other piece, she must have gone about in a ring, and come back again to where she first turned." The ring of invisibility, the circle of isolation which turns back on itself, the worm Ouroboros eating its own tail—all are images of infinity and self-consumption. It is Birdalone's task, and Morris's to break the circle, but the alienation which has thus far kept Birdalone alone and left the landscape a perfect wasteland extends to her arrival at the Castle of the Quest. Here she is told no women are allowed, but she suspects that the knights she seeks (on the instigation of the three sisters) are there, and she spends the night in a cave to find out. The next morning, awakened by "birds beginning their first song," Birdalone leaves the womb-like cavern to see her first glimpse of man in the approaching "glitter of spear-heads." Only after her arrival at the Castle of the Quest does she truly shed the childishness of psychological narcissism, homosexuality, and incest through which she has passed. She abandons the borrowed clothes she has worn since the Isle of Increase Unsought (a wonderfully paradoxical name), and receives new clothes of her own from the men. The knights costume her as a Lady (far above her inherited "social station"), and she assumes a new role of "Abiding" while the knights enact their own part in her complicated liberation process.

The Days of Abiding prove to be terribly uncomfortable. She has been outfitted in a manner to which she is not accustomed and left with no work to do. One senses in her bodily impatience a suggestion of the discomfort Morris himself must have felt as his decline in health made it more and more difficult for him to work. By the time he was writing this section of the narrative, his own life was becoming increasingly confined. Birdalone begins to learn how to read and write—direct means of entering a new mode of consciousness—and does a good deal of fine embroidery. Even so, the weight of idleness is too heavy for her, as it must have been for many Victorian women, particularly when accompanied by recently awakened yet unsatisfied sexual longings: "And she stayed her weeping, and was calmer. But still she walked the floor, and whiles looked out of window, and whiles she looked on her limbs, and felt the sleekness of her sides, and she said: O my body! how thou longest!"

She finally hears of the Stony People, who may grant her her greatest desire, and the interlude provides Morris the opportunity of introducing a wonderful folk-tale as sub-plot. The Greywethers are giants of past ages, embodying another version of the death in life motif. Their story is a particularly impressive allegory when read with the rise of historicism in mind; the historical consciousness of the late nineteenth century, fostered by Arnold, Ruskin, Darwin, Wells, and Morris himself, had both destructive and constructive aspects. These monuments of history are both threatening and informative, for they represent yet another means for transcending the isolation of the self. But Birdalone ignores the advice of Leonard, the narrator of this interlude, and is instead distracted and led astray by the Black Knight. She plays the coquette, and her trifling, though psychologically understandable, leads immediately to the death of three men: the Black Knight is killed by the Red Knight; the Golden Knight is slain by the Red Knight; and finally the Red Knight is dispatched by Hugh

55

the Green Knight. The recovery of Birdalone is paid for by great loss, and the violence of the passage describing these deaths is unmatched by anything since the early tales.

The way to conclusion and renewal begins with a ritual telling of her own story, a tale which Birdalone must reveal to all the assembly, though she desires to share it privately only with Hugh and Veridis. The psychological function is to bring the unconscious experience before the public consciousness; or, in Christian terms, a public confession. Hugh finally determines "to bring the matter to an end," and proves his masculinity, naked, in the witch's bed, when he overpowers her and seizes her magic elixir. This conquest in turn reveals the secret of invisiblity which has been the great source of power for the Isles of Increase Unsought (a societal parallel with industrial technology in the British Isles). The plenteous service and endless luxury of the land, it seems, was accomplished through deception and exploitation, and through the thralldom of women. The women explain their sensations under the influence of the elixir, and their account resembles the experience of Birdalone when she was transformed into the hind. The use of a drug by Morris is a characteristic device of fantasy, paralleled in stories such as *Snow White*, *Brave New World*, and *Island*, often as an instrument of repression. The incident once again serves as a reminder that the novel strives to integrate social and individual consciousness free from illusion or duplicity.

The final episodes are equally complicated and provocative, but too numerous to explore in detail. Birdalone finally meets her own mother, and only after her mother's death does she realize that she must complete the circle of her own journey to break completely from the repetitive cycles which are the single woman's role: "I must end the other deal of my journey bird-alone, as my name is," she tells Gerard and his sons. The return is rich in symbol, tending to reverse the effect of the first cycle: she no longer flaunts her newly-discovered sexuality but reverses it, making the journey in a costume in which "she might well pass for a young man, slender and fair-faced." The Isles of Increase Unsought are now a wasteland; the Sending Boat disappears, and Birdalone once more takes to the waters on her own. She strips herself of "all her raiment, till she was as naked as when she first came aland there that other time." The scene recalls her first swim toward escape, "If I might only swim all the water and be free," but she has grown stronger by the end of the book: "On swam Birdalone, not as one who had a mind to drown her for the forgetting of troubles, but both strongly and wisely." When her strength begins to fail, she is saved by a floating tree (the action parallels the conclusion of *Well*, with a wet tree replacing the Dry Tree); clinging to it she floats ashore.

Birdalone is back where she started, and when she steps onto the island "her flesh quaked indeed with the memory of bygone anguish, but valiantly she arose and faced the dwelling of the witch despite her naked helplessness." She finds her former mistress dead and buries her. Then she discovers the disintegrating remains of the Sending Boat, and has a vision there of the dread and wingless enemy of bird or woman: "She saw a stir about the stem which lay furthest in up the creek, and while she quaked with failing heart, lo! a big serpent, mouldy and hairy, grey and brown-flecked, came forth from under the stem and went into the water and up the bank and so into the dusk of the alderwood." The symbolic snake departs the waters of unconsciousness, no longer brandishing its threat of death or purely physical temptations of forbidden knowledge.

The following morning at the living tree, the Oak of Tryst, Birdalone once more meets her Woodmother, who clothes her in pure fairy garments and leads her to Arthur, who has been stripped to an unprotected natural state, "his head bowed down on to his knees and his face covered within his hands; he was clad but in two or three deerskins hung about him." In a terrifying scene, Arthur's suffering restores his innocence and lifts him beyond it: "Then he went down on his knees to her, and he also joined his hands to pray to her; but it seemed as if she was stricken to stone, so wholly she moved not. But for him, he sank his forehead to earth, and then he rolled over and his limbs stretched out, and his head turned aside and blood gushed out from his mouth."

Water is not only the wettest, it is also the bloodiest of Morris's fantasies. The blood of the characters is an expression of both passion and suffering, and whether it is shed to navigate the Sending Boat, or to purify and ritually unite the unconscious forces in the archetypal drama, the symbol is effectively wielded by Morris. The hero is made to bow down to the woman, to place his head upon Mother Earth, and the blood which flows from his mouth echoes the pain of the woman in birth and the blood which Birdalone has shed to undertake her liberation. The Woodmother stops the blood and restores Arthur to health.

Liberated from guilt and temptation (the serpent departed), Arthur and Birdalone each have shared a symbolically androgynous experience—Birdalone returning in male attire; Arthur in his obeisance and flowing blood. Together they can face a transformed world—or can themselves transform it. They return through the forest of Evilshaw "on the green road" through Greenford. Their decision to go to Utterhay is an action of high significance for Morris, who clearly identifies his "utter" sites as places of grave social evil. *Water* concludes with the optimistic view that society can be transformed through the integration of the psyche; and, as Morris seems to suggest in the rich green abundant at the book's end, social revolution (the budding of the new society) can occur only after effective personal liberation.

THE SUNDERING FLOOD

During the final eight years of his life, William Morris shaped and formed the adult fantasy novel, penning ten novels of lasting artistic and thematic strength. The most influential followers in his tradition, particularly C. S. Lewis and J. R. R. Tolkien, have gratefully acknowledged his contribution. While it is fair to say that *Water* is his last fully-realized work, *The Sundering Flood*, which he dictated literally from his death bed, combines and crystallizes the thematic conclusions of his major fiction.

The map which faces page one of *The Sundering Flood* gives a concrete visual chart of the realm of fantasy that Morris's characters inhabited from the first novel. All the terrains with which we have become familiar are designated— the city and the great sea that borders it, the Sundering Flood itself which sweeps through the midst of the city to penetrate the whole land, the Wood Masterless, the Desert Waste, Dale Country, and the Great Mountains which form the outer boundary on the map. The hero of the novel, or at least its most encompassing presence, is the body of the earth itself, and it includes all aspects of primitive naturalism associated with the fertile earth-goddesses of the earlier tales. The first chapter of the story is given over entirely to a detailed and loving portrait of the land, and much of the book's narrative action is determined by forces stemming from the earth.

This final fantasy demonstrates a vital secularism, humanism, and socialism of the highest order. It unfolds a redemptive vision that flies in the face of the "mass-hackled priest," presenting a confident balance of opposites and a unity-

in-discord beyond the fluctuations of dialectic or cyclic recurrence. The earthly millennium is approached in a very ordinary way—through love. More important than the union of hero and heroine is the unity that each feels with the natural world, a unity Morris predicted in *News From Nowhere* when he spoke of the "overweening love of the very skin and surface of the earth on which man dwells, such as a lover has in the fair flesh of the woman he loves; this, I say, was to be the new spirit of the time."
be the new spirit of the time."

The setting of *Flood* is the home called "Wethermel," "the last house but one. . . toward the mountains." There the orphaned Osberne has been cared for by his grandparents and an old woman of the house. In their superstitious oversimplification of life, the folk have divided the world into cycles of good and evil, even going so far as to assign good luck to one generation and bad luck to the subsequent one. Osberne's luck is expected to be good, and Morris allows that promise to fulfill itself to the point where the simple dichotomous thinking is eventually overcome. Beginning with a youthful hero even younger than the innocent Birdalone, Morris portrays in his final novel a vision of youth overcoming the divided nature of psychology, and the oversimplified morality of narrow, inherited assumptions about the way things must be. As in the earlier novels, the strongly divided aspects of the book can be seen as a humanly-embodied Marxian dialectic, but Morris consistently, and especially in this last work, seems to depart from Marx in several points. First, he does not attribute the divisions to a purely economic law, but sees them having roots in superstition, human sexuality, and psychology. Second, the conflict of thesis and antithesis is not seen to be an inevitable sequence of events, but one which can be broken by individual action, not necessarily by societal revolution. And finally, rather than promulgating an antithetical attitude in his works, Morris always moves toward harmonious synthesis or integration, a harmony in which human love and love for the earth itself are clearly involved in the dimension of spirit (the presence of magical elements often associated with the familiar Mother Earth is used to extend the spiritual dimension), rather than the material ownership of resources and the more mundane sphere of daily toil.

Osberne's sense of reality expands when he finds a strange new playmate in a cave: this curious friend "took a stone and stroked it, and mumbled, and it turned into a mouse, and played with us nought afraid a while; but presently it grew much bigger, till it was bigger than a hare; and great game me seemed that was, till on a sudden it stood on its hind-legs, and lo it was become a little child, and O, but so much littler than I; and then it ran away from us into the dark, squealing the while like a mouse behind the panel, only louder. Well, thereafter, my playmate took a big knife, and said: 'Now, drudgeling, I shall show thee a good game indeed.' And so he did, for he set the edge of the said knife against his neck, and off came his head; but there came no blood, nor did he tumble down, but took up his head and stuck it on again, and then stood crowing like our big red cock."

The cave, of course, echoing the caves in other novels, is symbolically the womb of Mother Earth. Human history begins in caves, and there is a suggestion in this tale, as we move with Osberne from the cave to the city, that we are progressing through many evolutionary stages in man's historical development. More importantly, this episode is the beginning of Osberne's initiation rites. In her study of "Myth and Ritual in the Last Romances of William Morris," Carole Silver points out that Morris was strongly influenced by anthropological studies of mythology which proliferated at the end of the century. Morris had been drawn to mythic sources by instinct; his interest in the writings of the

Grimm brothers and of Max Muller influenced nearly all of the romances. Another major influence was George Frazer, who published his findings on *Totemism* in 1887 and the first edition of *The Golden Bough* in 1890. Silver also speaks of the importance of Lewis H. Morgan's *Ancient Sorcery* (1887), for "Morgan's ideas shaped one of the works Morris valued most highly, Frederick Engels' *Origin of the Family, Private Property and the State* (1884)"; another author, E. B. Taylor, used the comparative method to argue the "thesis that cultures pass through the same stages of development, so that one may study modern primitive societies to understand ancient civilizations," an exploration that "greatly influenced Morris's friend and admirer, Andrew Lang." It was Lang, in fact, who "challenged Max Muller's view of the sun as the source of all nature myths. Instead, Lang found the roots of myth in vegetative and fertility cults, in early religion and magic."

The Roots of the Mountains makes these roots clearer than any of the previous works, and in it Morris makes the conclusions more distinctively his own. Silver points out that the early novels represent almost an historical, literal version of the anthropological conclusions being reached by contemporary researchers. But while Engels carries Marxism further in the direction of determinism and dialectical strategy for revolution, Morris, continued to develop in the role of social and humanist visionary. It is partly for this reason that his social and political writing is now gaining renewed attention as a new generation discovers the difference between Morris and doctrinaire (unimaginative) communist line. Mining the roots of myth, Morris asserted that they might hold ancient insight into the human consciousness, an insight more profound than the simple Marxist line which was colored so strongly by the temporary condition of society in the first throes of the industrial revolution.

When we see the child Osberne in his cave, witness to magical death and rebirth, we sense with him a power greater than life and death, one for whom there is no separation between head and body, thought and feeling—in short, a condition of consciousness beyond the dialectic. Osberne is exposed to heavy phallic symbolism in this initiation rite, including the knife the dwarf gives him, and the sword promised to him later in life. That Osberne should enter the womb to discover his phallic identity is not surprising; it represents an extension of the androgynous imagery of the earlier books, and echoes a common initiation described by Norman O. Brown in *Love's Body*: "The young man is put into a hole and reborn—this time under the auspices of his *male mothers*. Male mothers; or vaginal fathers: when the initiating elders tell the boys 'we two are friends,' they show them their subincised penis, artificial vagina, or 'penis womb'." The cutting off of the head suggests this sort of rite. And with this episode, Osberne is delivered over to his *male mothers*.

Wolves begin to prey upon the sheep, and the old man and Surly John, the hired assistant, are unable to deal with the problem. Young Osberne takes spear, shield, and his dwarf-given knife, and returns with three grisly trophies: "And stooping to his bag he drew out something and cast it on the board, and lo the sheared-off head of a great grey wolf with gaping jaws and glistening white fangs, and the women shrank before it." This incident occurs when the lad is twelve years old; the reader can only assume that his initiation in the cave and the knife he received there have equipped him to meet and subdue brute forces. Shortly after this, Osberne is attracted to another earthly shape, "two little knolls rising from the field." The landscape suggests breasts, and indeed this is a spot called Hartshaw Knolls where a widow lives with her daughter. An instinctive attraction of Osberne for the daughter, Elfhild, develops in the story, though they are separated by the Sundering Flood, the great gulf of unconscious flow which seems impassable. Elfhild, whose name suggests "dwarf-child," is likewise in touch with the earth; she too has received mysterious gifts, in a cave, and is acutely aware of the inevitable attraction between male and female, while being equally cognizant of their historical circumstances: "Yet this I find strange in thy song almost to foolishness, that thou speakest in it as I were a woman grown, and thou a grown man, whereas we be both children. And look, heed it, what sunders us, this mighty Flood, which hath been from the beginning and shall be to the end."

This great divisive force, however, is clearly less ancient than the earth forces which have taken a shaping role in the relationship. Osberne is next nurtured by the mysterious Steelhead, who conducts what is clearly a pagan baptism and laying on of hands. Steelhead, with a name which associates itself with the beheading tricks of the dwarf and with mature male sexuality, tells Osberne, "I must needs see thee naked if I am to strengthen thee as I am minded to do." They both strip, and in a scene which parallels the meeting of Birdalone and Habundia, "Steelhead called the lad to him all naked as he was, and said: 'Stand thou before me, youngling, and I will give thee a gift which shall go well with Boardcleaver [the sword].' And the lad stood still before him, and Steelhead laid his hands on the head of him first, and let them abide there a while; then he passed his hands over the shoulders and arms of the boy, and his legs and thighs and breast, and all over his body; and therewith he said: 'In our days and the olden time it was the wont of fathers to bless their children in this wise; but for thee, thy father is dead, and thy nighest kinsman is little-hearted and somewhat of a churl. Thus then have I done to thee to take the place of a father to thee, I who am of the warriors of while agone.' "

The events of the book, too numerous and complicated to detail here, follow the maturation of Osberne in the historical evolution of society. His early years are filled with battle and the exercise of a strength which eventually assures his triumph and his joining to Elfhild. The book demonstrates a truly amazing parallelism in its construction. The first thirty-two chapters deal with life in the Dale, where Elfhild and Osberne first realize their separate-but-joined lives (they are even the same age); after both of them have descended and re-emerged from the caves, they begin to draw together. In Chapter 32 Osberne finds the "Foemen Among the West Dalers" and discovers that Elfhild has disappeared. There are eight transitional chapters during which he decides to leave the Dale and find a new master. Then follow the twelve chapters of Osberne's adventures. In Chapter 52 Osberne meets Elfhild; then there are twelve chapters which provide for the telling of Elfhild's tale as they return as strangers to the Dale. This completes a second unit of thirty-two chapters. The book concludes with four chapters involving both characters, in which they make themselves known to their people. The organization is all in multiples of four—a number associated numerologically with the earthly quaternity, and one that governs the book from Osberne's initial household of four to his final meeting with Steelhead "once in every quarter."

Episodes are carefully balanced and one has the impression that the symmetry would have been even greater if Morris had lived long enough to revise his draft. The union of Osberne and Elfhild is the center, not the climax of the book. It is a significant departure not only from the pattern of Morris's earlier fantasies, but also a break from the romance tradition which postpones the union for the end. The implied social metaphor is that the antithetical forces of society can be reconciled within history, not at the end of the process, and the results of the union realized on earth, not in some mythical heaven.

The characters of Morris's fantasy prevail only partly through their own

60

achievements. They are victorious because they have become one with an archetypal structure, represented in the extensive guidance and influence of the Earth-women in the earlier novels, or of Steelhead and the wise magical woman in this final story—and all of them in turn embody ancient forces of the land itself. Morris's notes for his ending read insistently, "Steelhead at end," and the story's conclusion, dictated by Morris from his deathbed, makes it clear that Steelhead exemplifies a principle of eternal continuity. It is a bond of trust and personal ritual associated with the seasonal eternal return in the conclusion: "It is further to be told that once in every quarter Osberne went into that same dale wherein he first met Steelhead, and there he came to him, and they had converse together; and though Osberne changed the aspect of him from year to year, as for Steelhead, he changed not at all, but was ever the same as when Osberne first saw him, and good love there was between those twain."

This is a lesson repeated from *The Water of the Wondrous Isles*, where Habundia has the couple arrange a similar meeting: "Swear to me never wholly to sunder from me; that once in the year at least, as long as ye be alive and wayworthy, ye come into the Forest of Evilshaw, and summon me. . . that we may meet and be merry for a while, and part with the hope of meeting once more at least." As Morris felt the presence of the Sundering Flood of his own death and the unconsciousness he so often associated with water, he seems almost to have written this last fantasy to stress once more his secular faith in the inherent continuity of the force he called the "Weird."

He conveys an increasing faith in the fortunate workings of the "Weird" on earth in the later novels, and his choice of this term, rather than the "determinism" of Marxism or "predestination" of Christianity or even the familiar "fate" of mythic tradition, speaks well for his effort to dissociate himself from established doctrinaire attitudes. Matters of doctrinal contention were behind Morris's decision to leave the Socialist League; matters of dogma were always annoying to him, since he clearly realized their unimportance. There is a secular strength and conviction in this final novel that man will triumph and endure, not because of divine intervention, but because it is in man's nature to be whole. One can almost see Morris himself in Steelhead's conversation with the hermit near the end of the tale, throwing off the chains of supernaturalism with the vigor of human capability:

> *"Go in peace, and God and Allhallows*
> *keep thee," said the hermit.*
> *"Well, well," said Steelhead, "we will not contend*
> *about it, but I look to it to keep myself." And therewith*
> *he strode off into the night."*

5. SOME CLOSING REMARKS

Morris was a master-craftsman in many media, and seemed instinctively to absorb and express the creative potential of each of the materials he handled. It was a complete understanding of the possibilities of fiction that led Morris to write fantasies. His need to use words to construct an art uniquely appropriate to verbal form inclined him to avoid a mere repetition of real and ordinary scenes. He chose to use his language to create new worlds, not merely to imitate the old. This aspect of his fictional achievement is surely one of the reasons other linguists, like Tolkien, have also been drawn toward fantasy and linguistic invention.

But the impulse to provide his readers with a glimpse of possible worlds beyond the world was part of Morris's spiritual and social idealism from the first. In his first-published fiction, "The Story of the Unknown Church," he told of the elaborate vision of the artist reaching out to create a monument to his loving ideal. In Morris's case, since he decided against a career in the church, "The Unknown Church" served as a fitting manifesto. He began in that story to create a church of his own, a world beyond the world, one enriched through the artistic process as a method of worship, and simultaneously one grounded in his hopes for the world. As E. P. Thompson observes in his biography of Morris, this was a feeling shared by Burne-Jones: "It was as if the human spirit was being driven to more and more remote regions, but was still struggling to keep alive. As Burne-Jones once declared: 'The more materialistic Science becomes, the more angels shall I paint.' "

Art, and imagination exercised in art, are ways of coming close to the sense of creation the idea of God must signify; they became Morris's personal method of renewal, a method he hoped might renew the world. He published his fantasy writings in beautifully-designed editions from the Kelmscott Press, printed on the finest handmade paper, lavished with love and decorative attention, to be left as enduring monuments and models while his cheap-paper socialist tracts are mouldering into dust. The master mason of the unknown church gained immortality through the artistic expression of his imagination in his carvings, not through a salvation promised by conventional religious (or Marxist) doctrine. The framework, the construction of the church itself, Morris reminds us, is accomplished by the labor of many individually creative lives, and is properly understood only as an embodiment of imaginative energy. Energy directed toward creative worship is undying. In it we see and read the hand and hope of man.

SELECTED CRITICAL SOURCES

BIOGRAPHY

Philip Henderson, *William Morris: His Life, Work and Friends* (New York: McGraw-Hill, 1967).

J. W. MacKail, *The Life of William Morris* (London: Longmans, Green & Co., 1901).

E. P. Thompsen, *William Morris: Romantic to Revolutionary* (New York: Pantheon, 1977).

CRITICISM

Jessie Kocmanova, "The Aesthetic Purpose of William Morris in the Context of His Late Prose Romances," in *BRNO Studies in English*, Vol 6, 109, 1966. (Spisy filsoficke fakulty, Grohova. 7 Brno, Czechoslavakia).

C. S. Lewis, "William Morris," in *Rehabilitations and Other Essays* (Oxford, 1939).

Richard Mathews, *An Introductory Guide to the Utopian and Fantasy Writing of William Morris* (London: William Morris Centre, 1976).

May Morris, *The Introductions to the Collected Works of William Morris*, 2 volumes, with a Preface by Joseph Riggs Dunlap (New York, 1973); or see the introductions to individual volumes of the *Collected Works*.

William Morris Society, *Studies in the Late Romances of William Morris*, with an Introduction by Frederick Kirchoff and essays by Blue Calhoun, John Hollow, Norman Kelvin, Charlotte Oberg, and Carole Silver.

Charlotte Oberg, *A Pagan Prophet: William Morris* (University of Virginia, 1978).

Norman Talbot, "Women and Goddesses in the Romances of William Morris," in *Southern Review* (Adelaide, Australia), Vol III, 4, 1969.

W. B. Yeats, "The Happiest of Poets" in *Ideas of Good and Evil* (London, 1903).

THE MILFORD SERIES:
Popular Writers of Today

A continuing series of 64-page critical studies of the major popular authors of our times. Praised by *Choice*, *Library Journal*, *Science-Fiction Studies*, *Algol*, and *Delap's F & SF Review*.

1. *Robert A. Heinlein: Stranger in His Own Land*, Second Edition, by George Edgar Slusser [$1.95]
2. *Alistair MacLean: The Key Is Fear*, by Robert A. Lee [$1.95]
3. *The Farthest Shores of Ursula K. Le Guin*, by George Edgar Slusser [$1.95]
4. *The Bradbury Chronicles*, by George Edgar Slusser [$1.95]
5. *John D. MacDonald and the Colorful World of Travis McGee*, by Frank D. Campbell, Jr. [$1.95]
6. *Harlan Ellison: Unrepentant Harlequin*, by George Edgar Slusser [$1.95]
7. *Kurt Vonnegut: The Gospel from Outer Space (Or, Yes We Have No Nirvanas)*, by Clark Mayo [$1.95]
8. *The Space Odysseys of Arthur C. Clarke*, by George Edgar Slusser [$1.95]
9. *Aldiss Unbound; The Science Fiction of Brian W. Aldiss*, by Richard Mathews [$1.95]
10. *The Delany Intersection; Samuel R. Delany Considered As a Writer of Semi-Precious Words*, by George Edgar Slusser [$1.95]
11. *The Classic Years of Robert A. Heinlein*, by George Edgar Slusser [$1.95]
12. *The Dream Quest of H. P. Lovecraft*, by Darrell Schweitzer $2.45]
13. *Worlds Beyond the World; The Fantastic Vision of William Morris*, by Richard Mathews [$2.45]
14. *Frank Herbert: Prophet of Dune*, by George Edgar Slusser [$2.45]
15. *Lightning from a Clear Sky; Tolkien, the Trilogy, and the Silmarillion*, by Richard Mathews [$2.45]
16. *I. Asimov: The Foundations of His Science Fiction*, by George Edgar Slusser [$2.45]
17. *Conan's World and Robert E. Howard*, by Darrell Schweitzer [Oct. 1978; $2.45]
18. *Against Time's Arrow; The High Crusade of Poul Anderson*, by Sandra Miesel [Oct. 1978; $2.45]
19. *The Clockwork Universe of Anthony Burgess*, by Richard Mathews [Oct. 1978; $2.45]

Other Borgo Press Publications:

a. *The Beach Boys: Southern California Pastoral*, by Bruce Golden [$1.95]
b. *The Attempted Assassination of John F. Kennedy*, a science fiction novel by Lucas Webb [$1.95]
c. *Up Your Asteroid! A Science Fiction Farce*, by C. Everett Cooper [$1.95]
d. *Hasan*, an original fantasy novel by Piers Anthony [$3.95]
e. *The Wings of Madness; a Novel of Charles Baudelaire*, by Geoffrey Wagner [$3.95]
f. *A Usual Lunacy*, an original SF novel by D. G. Compton [Oct. 1978; $3.95]
g. *Beware of the Mouse*; the first novel in The Mouse That Roared Series, by Leonard Wibberley [Oct. 1978; $3.95]

To order, please send a check or money order for the full amount, plus 50¢ postage and handling for each item ordered, to The Borgo Press, P.O. Box 2845 San Bernardino, CA 92406. California residents please add 6% sales tax